THE CRISES OF POWER

An Interpretation of United States Foreign Policy During the Kissinger Years

☆☆☆THE CRISES OF POWER AN INTERPRETATION OF UNITED STATES FOREIGN POLICY DURING THE KISSINGER YEARS

BY SEYOM BROWN

New York   Columbia University Press

Library of Congress Cataloging in Publication Data

Brown, Seyom.
  The crises of power.

  Includes bibliographical references and index.
  1. United States—Foreign relations—1969–1974.
2. United States—Foreign relations—1974–1977.
3. Kissinger, Henry Alfred.   I. Title.
E855.B76   327.73   79-15796
ISBN 0-231-04264-7

Columbia University Press
New York   Guildford, Surrey

10 9 8 7 6 5 4 3 2

For Sarah E. Brown

⭐☆☆CONTENTS

☆ ☆ ☆ PREFACE

While waiting for Henry Kissinger's memoirs, I had qualms about offering my interpretation of United States foreign policy during the Nixon and Ford administrations. The foremost authority on the subject would surely provide new information about the reasons for the international behavior of the U.S. government during his tenure—reasons that in large measure could only be surmised by the outside observer. Some of my surmises were bound to be contradicted by Kissinger's own retelling of events and his reconstruction of the philosophy of those in power.

Soon, I suspected, we would be overwhelmed by fresh Kissingerisms. With characteristic persuasiveness Kissinger himself would set the terms of the debate over the historical meaning of his years in office. But perhaps this was all the more reason to use the thinking space between two Kissinger eras (Kissinger as foreign policy official and Kissinger as contemporary historian) to work out my own preliminary appraisal—unaffected by the storm of pro- and anti-Kissinger polemics that would be unleashed on the day the first excerpts of his memoirs appeared in print.

I submit this early interpretation of the foreign policies of the Nixon and Ford administrations out of conviction that their meaning for America and the world should not be left only to Kissinger himself or to those who have been closely associated with him to interpret. The eight years of Kissinger's reign over U.S. foreign policy now belong to history. Increasingly, those whose profession is to discern the historical significance of the actions of their contemporaries will be offering their appraisals of the Kissinger era. Kissinger, to be sure, has admirable credentials for engaging in such historical interpretation. His academic writings on nineteenth-century European statesmen are models of detached but deeply penetrating analysis. But his credentials for a similarly detached evaluation of his own role are somewhat less credible, especially in view of his evident inclination to seek elective office. The accounts of those who served with him also must be imbibed with a healthy dose of skepticism—whether they be the products of sycophants or of those now trying to get even for wounds to their careers or egos. Many of these memoirs will be indispensable documents, along with official records, for subsequent analysis of the Kissinger diplomacy; but a more complete understanding requires us to step back from the various insider accounts—incorporating them, yes, but also subordinating them to more detached analyses of the larger historical script from which the actors played their roles.

More than an academic understanding of recent history is involved. The ability of current and future designers and practitioners of U.S. diplomacy to serve the basic values of the nation depends crucially on the accuracy of their assessments of the main forces at work in the international system. What we can learn from Kissinger's attempts to manipulate and shape these forces can teach us much about their essential nature. For Kissinger, whatever his successes or failures during the Nixon and Ford administrations, was self-consciously trying to make a large impact on history.

Before becoming a public official he had written admiringly of statesmen who "seek to mold reality in light of their purposes" as distinguished from those who merely "adapt their purposes to reality."[1] In office, Kissinger frequently described his large purposes in vague but grandiose terms, and his tenure as a public official an opportunity to help transform the international system. "I feel we are at a watershed," he told Bill Moyers in a television interview. "We are at a period of extraordinary creativity or a period when really the international order came apart politically, economically, and morally. I believe that, with all the dislocations we now experience, there also exists an extraordinary opportunity to form for the first time in history a truly global society carried by the principle of interdependence. And if we act wisely and with vision, I think we can look back to all this turmoil as the birth pangs of a more creative and better system. If we miss the opportunity, I think there's going to be chaos."[2]

The objective of this essay is not to denigrate the Kissinger performance by holding it up to the expressed purposes of his statesmanship. The fact that he may have fallen short of his goals is, to my mind, compensated for by his having aimed higher than most of his contemporaries would have dared, and—I believe—also accomplished more. Rather, the effort here is only an attempt to help further understanding of the requirements of a foreign policy capable of advancing U.S. interests and the welfare of humankind in the current world situation.

In the failures of those who have aimed for the stars are the ingredients of future, perhaps more successful, efforts.

I am unable to acknowledge, as is the fashion, an impressive list of readers and consultants to enhance the credibility of this essay. This has been entirely an individual effort, working from published materials already available to the general public. It is a personal interpretation of these materials and of the domestic and international context of significant events of recent history. Thus I can truly say that no one but I—and my impatience to get on with the task of extracting the larger meaning of these materials and events—is to blame for any inaccuracies or omissions of important facts.

I do wish to acknowledge, however, the indispensable assistance of Kathryn Gelner in the preparation of the manuscript, and the encouragement and editorial supervision of Bernard Gronert and his staff at Columbia University Press. Finally, a word of special appreciation to my wife, Martha, whose intellectual and other stimulating interventions kept me from being corrupted by Dr. Kissinger's aphorism that "power is the ultimate aphrodisiac"; and to my two youngest sons, Benjamin and Matthew, who would not let me forget that the past is prelude more than prologue.

THE CRISES OF POWER

If you act creatively you should be able to use crises to move the world towards the structural solutions that are necessary. In fact, very often the crises themselves are a symptom of the need for structural re-arrangement.

—Henry A. Kissinger, 1974

1

☆ ☆ ☆ THE INHERITED FOREIGN POLICY CRISIS

> My own attitude toward crisis is best expressed in the way the word "crisis" is written in the Chinese language. Two characters are combined to form the word: One brush stroke stands for "danger" and the other character stands for "opportunity."
>
> Richard M. Nixon, in his Preface to the 1968 edition of *Six Crises* *

United States foreign policy was in crisis when Henry A. Kissinger assumed office in January 1969 as President Nixon's Special Assistant for National Security Affairs. Profound disorientation over the country's international purposes and the means to achieve them pervaded the foreign policy bureaucracy, Congress, and the elements of the public that are usually attentive to foreign policy matters. The bipartisan foreign policy consensus that had sustained vigorous executive action through two decades of the cold war had disintegrated.

Many officials and analysts whose lives had been devoted to international relations were leaving the field to concentrate on domestic problems—race relations, urban affairs—having had their fill of attempting to reconstruct the world in the image of America. Among the exiles from the Kennedy and Johnson administrations who remained interested in foreign affairs, most seemed mainly anxious to prevent the United States from repeating the errors that had led to the Vietnam fiasco. Working through the Democratic-controlled Congress, nongovernmental think tanks, and public interest lobbies, the repentant global ac-

* Pyramid Books, 1968, p. xx.

tivists now constituted a loose but powerful coalition for a highly restricted definition of U.S. interests, low defense budgets, and close congressional control over executive actions that could involve the country in international conflict.

As Nixon and Kissinger saw it, nothing less than the power of the United States was at stake—which to them meant that virtually everything was at stake. The realpolitik approach to international relations views power itself as the most vital of national interests. Power, like the human body's central nervous system, provides the essential capacity to ward off threats, satisfy basic needs, and realize other purposes. Even survival itself is meaningless without power, for without it one is a mere vegetable for others to manipulate.

National "power" to Nixon and Kissinger was never simply military power (although some of Kissinger's preofficial writings might have appeared to establish such an equation).[1] It was more generic than that, being the sum of the nation's capacities to act purposefully in international affairs and to resist being controlled by others. To be powerful, a country had to be able to provide or deny others what they wanted but could not obtain elsewhere.

The crisis of American power, as perceived by Nixon and Kissinger, was in large measure caused by psychological deficiencies rather than material ones. It emanated primarily from a collapse of confidence, both at home and abroad, in the U.S. government's capacity to effectively marshal this country's assets in support of its international interests.

From this perspective the restoration of America's power required, first, a liquidation of the Vietnam conflict in a way that would avert a dangerous polarization of American society and still preserve the reputation of the United States as a country that sustained its commitments; second, a realistic reordering of the nation's priority interests so as to avoid squandering its resources in the service of idealistic goals peripheral to the central balance of military and geopolitical power; third, the development of a concept of international order that—while consistent with the priority interests of the United States—would provide a standard of legitimacy to which most nations could attach themselves; and finally, purposeful and dramatic action on global issues so that this country's leaders, once again, would be looked to as the main pace setters in the international arena.

Nixon and Kissinger regarded the termination of U.S. military involvement in Vietnam as a prerequisite for fulfilling the other requirements for restoring U.S. power. While still trapped and bleeding in an Indochinese quagmire largely of its own making, the United States could hardly be considered as acting according to a rational strategy to implement its priority interests. Nor could it, while employing its advanced military equipment in a civil war in a remote poor country, credibly champion a standard of international order based on notions that the strong should not bully the weak and that force should not be employed across national boundaries to advance ideological objectives. The U.S. government, of course, still retained the capacity to act vigorously on various international matters of moment, and did so in some situations with effectiveness and flair; yet as long as U.S. leaders revealed profound impotence and irrationality in the face of the Vietnam conflict, their authority, and that of the U.S. government generally, would continue to erode at home and abroad.

The U.S. retreat from Vietnam, however, would have to be "honorable"—meaning that it would have to be a negotiated exit involving concessions by the North Vietnamese and their Soviet and Chinese backers. "However we got into Vietnam," Kissinger wrote in a January 1969 *Foreign Affairs* article outlining his terms for a settlement, "ending the war honorably is essential for the peace of the world. Any other solution may unloose forces that would complicate the prospects for international order."[2] Some of the forces feared by Kissinger and Nixon were international—militant revolutionaries emboldened to imitate Ho Chi Minh's defiance of the capitalist superpower; and Soviet and Chinese hardliners, now vindicated in their supposition that the West was too decadent, disorganized, and spineless to persist in foreign struggles that were protracted and costly. Some of the forces feared by the new administration were domestic—the anger of families whose sons had been killed or maimed for the patriotic objective of resisting the spread of communism; the military and their hawkish supporters in Congress, who would blame the foreign policy "establishment" for putting paralyzing limitations on the capabilities of U.S. military forces to smash the enemy; and a general explosion of fierce resentment by ordinary proud Americans at leaders who could not save the country from a humiliating defeat. A wave of Marxist revolutions abroad and a neofascist backlash at home—the worst of all possible worlds.

Convinced that it was insane to continue wasting American blood and treasure in a remote war against an enemy fighting for what it believed to be its national integrity, but equally convinced that it was an act of political suicide to "bug out" of Indochina, the Nixon administration prolonged the bloodshed for four years while it engaged in a diplomatic charade to preserve American honor, whose ultimate result was to devalue the meaning of honor itself. To the extent that a country's power is in part dependent on the honor of its government, the Nixon administration's Vietnam withdrawal policy (described in chapter 3) was bound to leave the country less powerful than it was before 1969.

The second requirement for a restoration of America's power—a more realistic definition of U.S. international interests—was now recognized as necessary throughout the policy community in order to avoid future Vietnams, to avoid having U.S. actions controlled by commitments that were the products of an American universalism no longer appropriate to the complicated world of the 1970s.

In the first of his four annual reports to Congress on U.S. foreign policy, President Nixon announced that his administration had instituted "a new approach to foreign policy, to match a new era of international relations." The approach bore the unmistakable imprint of its principal author, Henry Kissinger.

"The postwar period in international relations has ended," asserted the President. The ravages of World War II had been overcome. "Western Europe and Japan have recovered their economic strength, their political vitality, and their national self-confidence." The new nations too had less need to be as totally dependent on the United States, as previous administrations had assumed. "Once many feared that they would become simply a battleground of cold war rivalry and fertile ground for Communist penetration. But this fear misjudged their pride in their national identities and their determination to preserve their newly won sovereignty." In addition, the nature of the communist world had changed—"The power of individual Communist nations has grown, but international Communist unity has been shattered . . . by the powerful forces of nationalism." Meanwhile, "a revolution in the technology of war has altered the nature of the military balance of power . . . Both the Soviet Union and the United States have acquired the ability to inflict unacceptable damage on the other, no matter which strikes first. There can be no gain and certainly no victory for the power that provokes a thermonuclear exchange."[3]

If these trends were now taken fully into account, the foreign policy crisis inherited by the administration could be transformed into an opportunity to reformulate the international interests of the United States in a way that would match U.S. commitments to its capabilities. Kissinger had provided a broad-brush outline of the basis for a new concept of U.S. interests in his 1968 essay for the Brookings Institution. The essay was more precise in its characterizations of where we had been ("an undifferentiated globalism") than in its map of where we should be going, for as Kissinger put it, "in the years ahead, the most profound challenge to American policy will be philosophical: to develop some concept of order in a world which is bipolar militarily but multipolar politically."[4]

The new concept should relate U.S. interests to an understanding of historical trends, to an appreciation of the functions and limitations of national power in the international system, to the structural requirements for equilibrium in the contemporary setting. "But [this] philosophical deepening will not come easily to those brought up in the American tradition of foreign policy," wrote Kissinger. Foreign policy could no longer be based primarily on "enthusiasm, belief in progress, and the invincible conviction that American remedies can work everywhere."[5]

Anticipating what was soon to become the "Nixon doctrine"—although, ironically, when Kissinger wrote it he was foreign policy adviser to Nelson Rockefeller, then Nixon's main opponent for the Republican presidential nomination—Kissinger argued that

> the United States is no longer in a position to operate programs globally; it has to encourage them. It can no longer impose its preferred solution; it must seek to evoke it. In the forties and fifties, we offered remedies; in the late sixties and seventies our role will have to be to contribute to a structure that will foster the initiative of others. We are a superpower physically, but our designs can be meaningful only if they generate willing cooperation. We can continue to contribute to defense and positive programs, but we must seek to encourage and not stifle a sense of local responsibility. Our contribution should not be the sole or principal effort, but it should make the difference between success and failure.[6]

There were many target audiences for the Nixon doctrine—allies, adversaries, and the U.S. public—but significantly, its first official enunciation was on the Pacific island of Guam, a stopover during the President's round-the-world trip in the summer of 1969. Here, in a key staging area for the U.S. military effort in Vietnam, between Hawaii and the Chinese mainland, Nixon announced that the United States should not be expected to involve its own forces in future insurgency wars. The United States would furnish economic and military assistance where appropriate, but the nation directly threatened would have to provide the manpower for its own defense. However, the United States would provide a "shield" (presumably air power and naval support) if "a nuclear power threatens the freedom of a nation allied with us or of a nation whose survival we consider vital to our security and the security of the region as a whole."[7]

Kissinger's influence was evident here and was even more evident in the President's reiteration and explanation of the doctrine in his first State of the World message. Its "central thesis,"

Nixon told Congress, was "that the United States will participate in the defense and development of its allies and friends, but that America cannot—and will not—conceive *all* the plans, design *all* the programs, execute *all* the decisions, and undertake *all* the defense of the free nations of the world. We will help where it makes a real difference and is in our interest."[8]

The United States would honor its existing commitments, said the President, but henceforth "our interests must shape our commitments, rather than the other way around." New commitments would be undertaken only in light of "a careful assessment of our national interests and those of other countries, of the specific threats to those interests and of our capacity to counter those threats at acceptable risk and cost."[9]

The promised "careful assessment of our own national interests," however, never surfaced in the form of an official statement available to Congress and the public at large so that there could be agreed-upon terms of reference for assessing the worth and means of sustaining particular commitments. Consequently, what was supposed to be a new conceptual basis for reforging the shattered foreign policy consensus turned out to be a plea to Congress and to the public to trust the executive's wisdom in understanding what the national interest required. This, of course, Congress and the public were increasingly unwilling to do, especially as the commitments and tactics they were asked to support seemed more and more to imply a continuation of the universalistic pretentions to American omnipotence that Kissinger and Nixon had so eloquently criticized in their early statements. If there was to be a *selective* involvement in international events, the basis of the selections was to be formulated in the executive with a minimum of congressional participation; moreover, tremendous leeway for ad hoc, improvisatory international maneuvers was to be retained by the executive. This the Congress, backed by public opinion, was in no mood to allow, so what started out as a "philosophical" or "conceptual" crisis, in Kissinger's formulation, came close to being a constitutional crisis over the authority to conduct foreign policy that, when compounded by the constitutional crisis surrounding Watergate, almost completely sapped the country's capacity to act purposefully and credibly abroad.

Grandiose promises of conceptual innovation coupled with a confusing record of delivery also affected the administration's third imperative for restoring U.S. power—the development of a structure of international order consistent with U.S. interests. "The greatest need of the contemporary international system," wrote Kissinger in 1968, "is an agreed concept of international order."[10] Again, the Kissinger themes reappeared only slightly altered in President Nixon's first State of the World message:

> Peace must be far more than the absence of war. Peace must provide a durable structure of international relationships which inhibits or removes the causes of war. . . We are working toward the day when *all* nations will have a stake in peace, and will therefore be partners in its maintenance.[11]

The "structure of peace," as sketched in this initial Nixon administration statement, was supposed to have three "pillars": (1) "partnership," a euphemism for the Nixon doctrine's devolution of ground warfare and counterinsurgency responsibilities to U.S. allies; (2) "strength," a rationalization of U.S. military capabilities, particularly strategic forces, to preserve a global balance of military power and regional balances in the context of the Soviet Union's having attained essential strategic equality with the United States; and (3) "willingness to negotiate," a vague early formulation of what was soon to emerge as the triangular relationship of U.S.–Soviet détente on the one hand and the U.S.–China rapprochement on the other.[12]

The first two "pillars" hardly rated their advertisement as conceptual innovations, and the third—the promise of an "era of negotiation" to supplant the "era of confrontation"—remained little more than a tantalizing slogan until the surprising démarches toward China and the Soviet Union of 1971–1972. The billing *"structure* of peace" was particularly mystifying, for there was no accompanying design, or even outline, of the essential characteristics of the international order that was supposed to be produced by these policies.

There was considerable talk by Kissinger of giving the Soviets "a stake in the international equilibrium" in connection with the U.S.–Soviet agreements in and surrounding the 1972 Nixon–Brezhnev summit. Journalists and academics speculated that the equilibrium was supposed to result from the interplay of forces in a "pentagonal" structure, a five-sided balance of power reminiscent of eighteenth- and nineteenth-century European balances that Kissinger was thought to want to reinstitute. Clues to the unrevealed grand design were sought in oblique formulations such as the President's statement to *Time* magazine that "it would be a safer world and better world if we have a strong, healthy United States, Europe, Soviet Union, China, Japan; each balancing the other, not playing one against the other, an even balance."[13]

But it was left largely to unofficial commentators to infer the grand design behind particular policies. An October 1974 interview with the Secretary of State by James Reston of the *New York Times* reflected the general impatience with Kissinger's failure to clearly articulate his basic assumptions. "When you came to Washington . . . it was said that you had a concept of how to achieve order in the world," said Reston, "and yet . . . since you have been here, the tendency has been to say that you have not defined your concept, but that actually what you have been doing is negotiating pragmatic problems and not really dealing with the concept or making clear the concept. What is the concept?"

Kissinger's response was simply to deny the criticism and assert that when he and his associates tackle a problem, "we spend the greatest part of our time at the beginning trying to relate it to where America and the world ought to go before we ever discuss tactics."[14]

Later in the same interview, Reston pressed the Secretary once again to articulate his essential goals. The exchange illustrates Kissinger's mastery of the art of appearing to say more than he actually does:

RESTON: When you leave this office, what is it you want to have achieved at the end of your service?

KISSINGER: It used to be that the overwhelming concern of any President or Secretary of State had to be to make a contribution to peace in the traditional sense. That is to say, to reduce tensions among nations or regions. That remains, of course, an essential preoccupation. History has, I think, placed me in a key position at a time when we are moving from the relics of the postwar period toward a new international structure.

The Administration did not invent that structure. It did have, however, an opportunity to contribute to it—an opportunity that did not exist 10 years earlier and that may not exist 10 years later. Now, the difference between that structure and the previous period is that there are more factors to consider and that it has to be built not on the sense of the pre-eminence of two power centers, but on the sense of participation of those who are part of the global environment.

This has required a change in the American perception of the nature of foreign policy. What is described as excessive pragmatism is really a rather conscious attempt to try to educate myself, my generation, and my associates, insofar as I can contribute to living with the world as it is now emerging. Pragmatism unrelated to a purpose becomes totally self-destructive.

In addition, I would like to leave at least the beginning of a perception of a structure that goes beyond these centers of power, and moves towards a global conception. There is no question in my mind that, by the end of the century, this will be the dominant reality of our time. I believe we have to move towards it now.

RESTON: Can you define it?

KISSINGER: Before I go into that, let me say . . . [Here the Secretary of State began to talk of the difference between personal ambition to stay on the job and the need to accomplish something for the good of the country—never returning to Reston's question of how he would define his global conception.][15]

Others also tried to get Dr. Kissinger to be more forthcoming and precise in describing the "structural" characteristics of the future world order that he insisted was animating U.S. foreign policy during the Nixon and Ford administrations. During a thoughtful television interview of Kissinger, Bill Moyers recalled a conversation they had at Harvard six months before Nixon's inauguration. "You had a reasonably clear view, a map of the world in your mind at that time," said Moyers, "a world based on the stability brought about by the main powers. I'm wondering what the map is like in your mind now of the world." Once again, however, Kissinger restricted himself to a remarkably cryptic answer:

> Well, I thought at the time, and I still do, that you cannot have a peaceful world without most of the countries, and preferably all of the countries, feeling that they have a share in it. This means that those countries that can have the greatest capacity to make—to determine peace or war, that is, the five major centers—be reasonably agreed on the general outlines of what that peace should be like. But at the same time, one of the central facts of our period is that more than a hundred nations have come into being in the last fifteen years, and they too must be central participants in this process. So that for the first time in history foreign policy has become truly global, and therefore truly complicated.[16]

Dr. Kissinger appeared to know where he was sailing the ship of state; but if there *was* a map in his head, he was reluctant to share it with the passengers or even the crew. They all were supposed to have faith in Henry the Navigator. Increasingly, however, as some of his almost magically fashioned international arrangements began to unravel—SALT, economic détente, the Vietnam Peace Accords, step-by-step diplomacy in the Middle East—a willing suspension of disbelief was no longer possible for many of his former admirers. Perhaps his most disparaging critics were right, that the Kissinger phenomenon had more flair than philosophy, more shuttle than substance.

Yet the performance did at least *imply* some major premises about the emerging international order and about what the United States (or Henry Kissinger) could and should do to help shape it. Significantly, the actions and the implied assumptions approximated rather closely the guidelines for statecraft that Kissinger had articulated in his historical writings, as distinct from his writings on military strategy and foreign policy during the cold war. This suggests that the international and domestic changes of the middle and late 1960s took Kissinger by surprise, as they did most of his contemporaries, and that for his intellectual retooling he relied on analysis by historical analogy much more than he cared to admit.

The pertinent analogies came mostly from the nineteenth-century Concert of Europe rather than from the classical eighteenth-century Balance of Power system—a point missed by much of the academic criticism of Kissinger's policies, which tried to score points on the former professor by showing how different the contemporary world is from Europe in the eighteenth century. To be sure, the contemporary world is also very different from nineteenth-century Europe, as Kissinger himself has often pointed out;[17] but the essential lessons Kissinger the historian drew from the successes and failures of the great diplomats of the post-Napoleonic period are amazingly similar to the premises of the *weltanschauung* that can be inferred from Kissinger's own diplomacy.[18]

An international order that could contain the clash of national interests, power rivalries, and ideological antagonisms from engulfing world society in war, anarchy, and chaos had two structural imperatives, according to Kissinger: (1) an equilibrium of military power and (2) acceptance by the major powers of certain fundamental principles of legitimate and illegitimate state action in the international system. The substance of the requirements would vary in different historical epochs, but equilibrium and legitimacy would always be essential requisites for a civilized world. Neither was sufficient by itself. In the thermonuclear age they had become the twin conditions for the very survival of the human species.

History teaches, wrote Kissinger, "that no order is safe without physical safeguards against aggression."[19] States had to be ready and willing to apply military force to prevent any of their number from attempting to dominate the international system against the will of the others, or to violate its essential rules. Order thus required the capacity and the will, on the part of at least the major powers, to fight for more than one's immediate security. Commitments to weaker members of the system to help them fight against a country attempting to attain hegemony, and commitments to fight against aggression itself, were also necessary. To this extent at least, the lessons of history supported the basic containment and alliance policies of postwar U.S. administrations from Truman through Johnson.

For military containment to work, however, the will, on the part of those committed to order, to dispense with peace itself had to be made evident to those who might violate the rules of the system. There could be no military equilibrium—what in the contemporary period is called stable deterrence—without general confidence in its *psychological* as well as its physical components. As Kissinger put it,

> Whenever peace—conceived of as the avoidance of war—has been the primary objective of a power or a group of powers, the international system has been at the mercy of the most ruthless member of the international community. Whenever the international order has acknowledged that certain principles could not be compromised even for the sake of peace, stability based on an equilibrium of forces was at least conceivable.[20]

This was precisely what was so worrisome about the present period, and why military containment might now be insufficient.

Faced with the prospect of thermonuclear extinction, alliance partners who were themselves not directly under attack might too readily alter their principles rather than join the fight. Sensing this, a revolutionary superpower—one anxious to dominate or overturn the existing system—could be tempted to coercively exploit the weak links in a containment chain on the assumption that even the rival superpower would retreat from military engagement. This assumption, though, might turn out to be a gross miscalculation, and could bring on the terrible holocaust whose anticipation was supposed to have eroded the will to resist the revolutionary superpower's aggression. Thus, the equilibrium system under today's conditions, if based almost entirely on a balance of military power, not only would be insufficient to prevent threats to the existing order but might prove to be too unstable to prevent the outbreak of central war.

Because central war could mean the destruction of civilization, it was more crucial than ever before to supplement the system of military equilibrium with a system of political "legitimacy." Once again, Kissinger defines the essence of such a system in his major historical work on the nineteenth-century Concert of Europe:

> "Legitimacy" as here used should not be confused with justice. It means no more than an international agreement about the nature of workable arrangements and about the permissible aims and methods of foreign policy. It implies the acceptance of the framework of the international order by all major powers, at least to the extent that no state is so dissatisfied that, like Germany after the Treaty of Versailles, it expresses its dissatisfaction in a revolutionary foreign policy.[21]

But just as the military equilibrium was insufficient to preserve the peace, so legitimacy—general international acceptance of the existing order—was hardly by itself an adequate basis for restraining a revolutionary state determined to smash that order. Indeed, if the revolutionary state is powerful enough, the conditions for a legitimate international order are negated, for in such situations "it is not the adjustments of differences within a given system that will be at issue, but the system itself. Adjustments are possible, but they will be conceived as tactical maneuvers to consolidate positions for the inevitable showdown, or as tools to undermine the morale of the protagonist."[22]

It was clear from Kissinger's historical and policy-oriented writings before he became a public official that he considered the Soviet Union and China to be "revolutionary states"—states whose aspirations could not be satisfied by the international order insisted on by the other major powers—and that the Soviet Union, at least, was powerful enough to make it impossible to restore a system of international legitimacy. Yet the Nixon–Kissinger "structure of peace" assumed a positive Soviet stake in the emerging international order.

The Declaration of Principles signed by Nixon and Brezhnev at their 1972 Moscow summit meeting included promises by both superpowers to base their relations on the principles of "sovereignty, equality, noninterference in internal affairs and mutual advantage"; to "always exercise restraint in their mutual relations; to negotiate and settle differences by peaceful means"; and to refrain from attempts to gain "unilateral advantage at the expense of the other, directly or indirectly."[23] A large package of interrelated U.S.–Soviet negotiations on specific issues—arms, control, economic and technological cooperation, a Middle East peace, and rules of mutual nonintervention in the other power's sphere of influence and in third-area conflicts—were supposed to provide a web of relationships, each linked to all of the others, that the Soviet Union would have strong incentives not to unravel.[24]

Not surprisingly, some of Kissinger's critics on the right pointed to this basic "contradiction" in Kissinger's "grand design." Warren Nutter, an assistant secretary of defense for international security affairs during the Nixon administration, observed that whereas Kissinger had stressed in his scholarly writings that diplomacy vis-à-vis a revolutionary power could play only a symbolic role, "he now argues that negotiation with the Soviet Union will result in great substantive achievements."[25] Kissinger's main argument—that détente, even though it could not guarantee a modification of the Soviet Union's revolutionary aims, was a moral imperative in an age when thermonuclear war was the likely consequence of the failure to accommodate the conflicting aims of the superpowers—was lost on his critics.

Increasingly, during the Ford administration, the Reagan wing of the Republican party attacked the Secretary of State for giving the Soviet Union more than the United States got in return—in the SALT negotiations, in East–West commerce, and in the Helsinki Final Act of the Conference on Security and Cooperation in Europe. So virulent was the right wing criticism that in his 1976 campaign for the presidential nomination Ford explicitly renounced further official use of the word détente; and in the 1976 Republican National Convention the Reagan forces were able to insert anti-détente and anti-Kissinger planks in the platform.

Some liberals were angered by Kissinger's unwillingness to press the Soviet Union and other autocratic regimes on the sub-

ject of human rights. Kissinger's rationale for avoiding direct diplomatic pressure on the Soviet Union for its violations of human
rights, and his opposition to the congressional refusal to grant
commercial privileges and government credits to the USSR unless the Kremlin liberalized its restrictions on emigration, em-
phasized the risks to détente. Perhaps he was reluctant to voice
the deeper conceptual basis for such restraint for fear of having
his ideas appear too "classical" or European.

The result was not simply a conceptual void but also a tacit coalition among conservatives and liberals in opposition to Dr. Kissinger's alleged amoralism and supposed preference for negotiating with dictators rather than with genuine democrats. For
Kissinger's critics on the left, this presumed moral deficiency
was compounded by the blatant hypocrisy of professing noninterference in the domestic affairs of other states while authorizing antileftist activities by U.S. operatives in various countries—
the most notorious being the Central Intelligence Agency's aid to
anti-Allende forces in Chile.

In short, the world order concept, which was to provide a
vision capable of rallying not only a new domestic consensus but
also an international consensus, was revealed only in fragments,
coyly, and defensively. Those few who thought they caught a
glimpse of the larger concept were not at all sure they liked what
they saw. Others who listened to Kissinger's sonorous explanations of his policy initiatives doubted even the existence of a
larger concept behind the hyperactive diplomacy. The need to
restore confidence at home and abroad that the United States
was again capable of acting purposefully in the world was passed
on by Kissinger to his successors. Surely this must have been
one of his keenest personal disappointments. It was equally a
misfortune for the country, for he had correctly diagnosed the
need for conceptual clarification but was unable to provide the
remedy.

Because of Kissinger's reluctance to fully share the premises of
his actions with his domestic and international audience, his
performance during the eight years of the Nixon and Ford ad-

ministrations came off more as a brilliantly executed series of improvisations than as a "mosaic" (one of Kissinger's favorite terms) in which each of the parts is integral to the whole conception. The best improvisations, of course, do emanate from a concept underneath the apparent spontaneity at the surface, and this was in fact the case with Kissinger's most important moves: his negotiations with Le Duc Tho leading to the U.S. disengagement from Indochina; his simultaneous catering to Soviet and Chinese desires to increase their international respectability; his step-by-step diplomacy in the Middle East; his response to Third World economic demands at the Seventh Special Session of the United Nations; and his shift in the "tilt" of U.S. policy in Southern Africa, away from the support of white minority governments and toward the goal of black majority rule.

The fit of each of these tactical moves into Kissinger's grand strategy will be analyzed in subsequent chapters. Regardless of their substantive validity, however, they did serve as opportunities for Kissinger to "make waves," to recreate positive popular excitement around U.S. foreign policy, to restore America's existential leadership—characteristically based on the scope and momentum of this country's reaction to world events more than on depth of understanding. Although Kissinger had hoped to root U.S. foreign policy more deeply in a historically derived philosophy of international relations, he found himself turning into the arch practitioner of the razzle-dazzle, "can do" American pragmatism that he had previously condemned. Instead of the Europeanization of America, the world was treated to the Americanization of Henry.

Innovation, surprising changes of direction, a ubiquitous presence, sheer momentum itself—these Kissinger knew were important aspects of power; but he also knew that such an activist diplomacy, unless "in the hands of a master," could become mindless and risky.[26] It was important, therefore, for the innovator to *institutionalize* the premises of his policy before he left office, or else they might be dissipated by his successors. However, as crisis cascaded upon crisis and the activist style eclipsed the philosophical, there was little left to institutionalize except Henry Kissinger himself—which he had to admit (humorously, but perhaps seriously) was a tragic impossibility.

Kissinger identified with the imposing statesmen he wrote about—with their success, but also with their failures. At the end of one of his most eloquent historical essays, he quoted from a poignant Bismarck letter: "That which is imposing here on earth . . . has always something of the fallen angel who is beautiful but without peace, great in his conceptions and exertions but without success, proud and lonely." [27]

2

☆☆☆THE INSUFFICIENCY OF MILITARY CONTAINMENT

> What in the name of God is strategic superiority? What is the significance of it, politically, militarily, operationally, at these numbers? What do you do with it?
> Henry A. Kissinger in Moscow, 1974 *

Détente with the Soviet Union, rapprochement with China—both of these early démarches of the Nixon administration were to a large extent prompted by the realization that Soviet military power could now neutralize the ability of U.S. military power to deter objectionable Soviet behavior short of direct threats to the United States itself. New means for affecting Soviet behavior were required to supplement military deterrence.

Military power was still considered necessary to induce the Soviet Union to respect the range of U.S. interests abroad, for if the Soviet Union, but not the United States, were able and willing to resort to force when the secondary interests of the two superpowers clashed, the Soviets could face down the United States in situation after situation and ultimately achieve a position of global dominance. But U.S. military power was no longer deemed sufficient for containing the Soviet Union within its current sphere of dominance, for military containment was based on confidence that the United States would prevail in any major U.S.–Soviet war—a belief that was eroding by the late 1960s.

---

* News conference of July 3, 1974, *Department of State Bulletin*, no. 1831 (July 29, 1974), 71:215.

Confidence that the United States would prevail in U.S.–Soviet military encounters rested in some important cases on the credibility of U.S. threats to escalate a conflict to strategic levels, for example, in Berlin crises, where the Russians enjoyed a preponderance of locally applicable force. But now that the Soviet Union as well as the United States was supposed to have a strategic arsenal capable of assuring virtually total destruction of the attacker, no matter how large and well executed its first strike, it was highly unlikely that either superpower would seriously contemplate attacking the other for any purpose except retaliation for a direct attack on itself. With strategic deterrence thus restricted to the ultimate holocaust, lesser Soviet aggressive moves, even against loyal allies of the United States, could not be reliably prevented unless the United States and its allies developed other weighty levers on Soviet behavior.

The raw materials for fashioning such levers were sought by Nixon and Kissinger in the mutual paranoia between the Russians and the Chinese and in the Kremlin's desire to increase the Soviet Union's participation in the international economy. It was uncertain, however, that the contemplated triangular relationship—assuming that both communist powers, for their own reasons, would latch on—would indeed operate to dissuade the Russians and the Chinese from attempting to take advantage of the new mood of isolationism growing in the United States. And the expectation that expanded commercial contacts would provide substantial U.S. leverage on the Soviets was also still only a hypothesis.

Meanwhile, congressional efforts to reduce U.S. defense expenditures were intensifying, and this, if successful in the context of the Soviet military buildup, could shift the global military balance in favor of the Russians. Nixon and Kissinger, neither of whom had been enthusiasts of arms control before 1969, now felt compelled to seriously negotiate limitations on the arms race.

Arms control thereupon was added to expansion of commercial relations with the USSR and normalization of relations with Peking as the cornerstones of the "structure of peace" that President Nixon spoke of in his 1969 inaugural address. For Kissinger they became essential elements of global order that otherwise— owing to the inherent weakness of containment based mainly on military deterrence—would become dangerously unstable.

The Arms Control Dilemma

Putting a cap on the strategic arms race proved to be the most difficult of the international restructuring tasks that Nixon and Kissinger set for themselves. It required that both sides abandon the goal of strategic superiority and that each give up attempting to protect its population against the other's nuclear attack. The concepts of parity and mutual deterrence went against the grain of many of the influential military and foreign policy elites in both countries. Moreover, the esoteric strategic doctrine that mutual deterrence required both sides to protect their missiles but not their people was hardly likely to be popular with the general public.

Nixon himself, having frequently rejected strategic parity as an acceptable context for conducting U.S.–Soviet relations, and having promised during the 1968 election campaign to restore "clear-cut military superiority" as a planning objective, was not about to frontally contradict hopes in the Pentagon (now free from the planning constraints of the McNamara years) to once again pull well ahead of the Russians. The new Presidential Assistant for National Security Affairs, however, provided just the right conceptual finesse. At his first presidential news conference, Nixon was asked by a questioner to distinguish between the planning goal of superiority over the Soviet Union being propounded by Secretary of Defense Melvin Laird and a notion being advanced by Kissinger called "sufficiency." Nixon's answer, while leaving much to later elaboration, deftly chalked out the middle ground:

> I think the semantics may offer an appropriate approach to the
> problem. I would say, with regard to Dr. Kissinger's suggestion of

sufficiency, that that would meet certainly my guideline and, I think
Secretary Laird's guideline with regard to superiority.

Let me put it this way: When we talk about parity, I think we
should recognize that wars occur usually when each side believes it
has a chance to win. Therefore, parity does not necessarily assure
that a war may not occur.

By the same token, when we talk about superiority, that may
have a detrimental effect on the other side in putting it in an infe-
rior position and therefore giving great impetus to its own arms
race.

Our objective in this administration . . . is to be sure that the
United States has sufficient military power to defend our interests
and to maintain the commitments which this administration deter-
mines are in the interests of the United States around the world.

I think "sufficiency" is a better term, actually, than either "superiority" or parity."[1]

The new strategic planning concept, as elaborated in subsequent statements by the administration, was supposed to accomplish a number of purposes—not all of them compatible.

Sufficiency first and foremost required enough well-protected
strategic forces to be able to inflict a level of damage on the Soviet Union that would deter the Soviet leaders from attacking. In
this respect the Nixon administration incorporated the "assured
destruction" criterion of former Secretary of Defense Robert
McNamara. Assured destruction, however, was deemed insufficient as a force planning concept, for, as interpreted by Nixon,
it was "limited to the indiscriminate mass destruction of enemy
civilians as the sole possible response to challenges." This
would be an incredible response insofar as it involved "the likelihood of triggering nuclear attacks on our own population." As
such, it was an inadequate strategic basis for preventing the Soviets from coercing the United States and its allies.[2]

It was also essential, explained the President, to maintain "a
flexible range of strategic options." Given the variety of possible
politico-military situations that could conceivably confront us,
"our strategic policy should not be based solely on a capability
of inflicting urban and industrial damage presumed to be

beyond the level an adversary would accept. We must be able to respond at levels appropriate to the situation."[3]

However, this "flexible options" objective was to receive special articulation and emphasis by Secretary of Defense James Schlesinger during the second Nixon administration, to the point at which it endangered the arms *limitation* objective of the sufficiency doctrine, namely, that the deployments on either side should not appear to threaten the other with a disarming attack. In the jargon of defense planners, the flexible options objective opened the door to new "counterforce" weapons and improvements designed to limit the damage that Soviet strategic forces could inflict on the United States. Consequently, to the extent that American strategic forces were able to effectively perform this damage-limiting function, they would undermine the Soviet's assured-destruction capability and thus engender new Soviet force expansion programs.

The Nixon administration had three essential reasons for continuing such potentially destabilizing programs: (1) Deterrence *could* fail, and in such situations—however low their probability—the United States would want to disable as much of the Soviet war-fighting capability as possible, and to reduce the Soviet capacity to kill Americans. (2) The Soviets had been building an impressive counterforce capability that by the late 1970s or early 1980s might be able to destroy most of the U.S. land-based ICBMs; the clear strategic asymmetry that would be produced by the presence of such a Soviet capability and the absence of a comparable U.S. capability could be politically exploited by the Soviets in crisis confrontations between the superpowers. (3) The United States would be more effective in bargaining with the Soviets to alter and reduce the counterforce features of their strategic force programs if we too had counterforce elements that would need to be sacrificed; moreover, the existence of such U.S. programs would dramatize for the Soviets the consequences of a failure to agree to their limitation, namely, a counterforce arms race with the United States, whose technological abilities in this field were still far ahead of the Soviets'.[4]

The "flexible options" criterion thus was itself justified not only on narrow military grounds but also by the most elastic criterion of the administration's sufficiency doctrine. In President Nixon's words,

> The concept of sufficiency is . . . in part a political concept, and it involves judgements whether the existing and foreseeable military environment endangers our legitimate interests and aspirations. . . .
>
> In its broader political sense, sufficiency means the maintenance of forces adequate to prevent us and our allies from being coerced. Thus the relationship between our strategic forces and those of the Soviet Union must be such that our ability and resolve to protect our vital security interests will not be underestimated.[5]

But here was the persistent dilemma—once again unresolved though partially dissolved in a sea of ambiguous rhetoric—of how to keep the U.S. strategic deterrent umbrella extended over a broad range of U.S. alliance commitments and at the same time relinquish a strategic "first-strike" option against the Soviet Union. For, at base, the U.S. assurance to its allies that it would not allow them to be victimized by a Soviet threat to attack them with nuclear weapons rested on a readiness to issue a counterthreat to "retaliate" with a nuclear strike against the Soviet Union; such a "retaliation" would be in fact the first blow in a U.S.–Soviet war. Indeed, it was precisely the Soviet attainment in the late 1960s of an awesome intercontinental retaliatory capability that could absorb any first strike and still deliver a devastating response that seriously weakened the credibility of any U.S. threat to initiate a strategic nuclear war between the superpowers—even in response to a Soviet attack on Western Europe. If the United States and the Soviet Union were now explicitly to renounce first-strike capabilities against each other, the central ribbing of the NATO umbrella would collapse and Western Europe would be an exposed target for nuclear blackmail by the Kremlin.

Consequently, in order to shore up the credibility of its commitments to NATO, the United States continued to deploy weapons with an impressive potential for destroying Soviet offensive strategic missiles and to justify these deployments with the broad "political" aspects of the sufficiency doctrine. This was, of course, at considerable tension with the self-limiting aspect of the doctrine—in particular U.S. official insistences that

> sufficiency also means numbers, characteristics, and deployments of our forces which the Soviet Union cannot reasonably interpret as being intended to threaten a disarming attack.[6]

Considering the inherent cross-purposes of strategic arms control and the continued reliance on strategic weapons to protect U.S. allies against the Soviet Union, the ambiguity in the most carefully prepared administration statements surely must have been purposefully designed. Quoting again from the President's 1971 State of the World message,

> Defensive in its essence, the decision to pursue a policy of strategic sufficiency rather than strategic superiority does not represent any lessening of our resolve not to permit our interests to be infringed. The doctrine of sufficiency represents, rather, an explicit recognition of the changed circumstances we face with regard to strategic forces. The United States and the Soviet Union have now reached a point where small numerical advantages in strategic forces have little military relevance. The attempt to obtain large advantages would spark an arms race which would, in the end, prove pointless. For both sides would almost surely commit the necessary resources to maintain a balance.[7]

In addition, the Department of Defense seized upon Nixon's ambiguous concept of sufficiency to establish elastic definitions of what would constitute an adequate military balance of power vis-à-vis the Soviets. During the Kennedy–Johnson years Secretary of Defense McNamara had held down the U.S. strategic force posture with an increasingly strict application of the "assured-destruction" criterion, which he defined as being able to destroy one-quarter of the Soviet population and one-third of Soviet industry. No matter what the Soviets might deploy, it was sufficient to be able to inflict this level of damage in retaliation for a Soviet first strike in order to deter the Kremlin from launching a strategic attack. Now, under Secretary Laird, the military planning objectives were broadened to ensure that (a) the Soviet forces could not inflict substantially more damage in the United States than the U.S. forces could inflict on the USSR; (b) that each leg of the strategic "triad" (bombers, land-based ICBMs, and sea-based strategic missiles) would be independently able to survive a surprise Soviet attack and strike back with a society-destroying level of destruction; and (c) that, in addition to these war outcome criteria, the number of weapons deployed on each side should not *appear* to give the Soviet Union an advantage.[8]

Ambiguous rhetoric might obscure the contradictions between the Nixon–Laird notion of sufficiency as a defense planning concept and the Nixon–Kissinger concept of sufficiency as an armament-limiting concept; but when it came to actually negotiating a strategic arms limitation agreement with the Russians, one or the other had to be given the presidential nod. During the first Nixon administration, 1969–1972, Kissinger— partly through persuasion, partly through deft bureaucratic infighting, partly by setting the proper international events into motion—was able to gain Nixon's endorsement of his version at critical junctures.[9]

The climax of the first phase of the U.S.–Soviet strategic arms limitation talks (SALT), culminating in the Moscow agreements of 1972—the treaty limiting antiballistic missile (ABM) systems and the interim agreement on offensive strategic systems—came very close to institutionalizing a "mutual assured destruction" relationship, dubbed MAD by its critics.

According to Article I of the ABM treaty, "Each party undertakes not to deploy ABM systems for a defense of the territory of its country."[10]

The limited deployments allowed by the treaty (Article III) restricted each side to two sites of 100 launchers each, one site to protect an offensive missile field and the other to protect the country's capital.[11] Clearly, the populations of both countries were to remain unprotected, consistent with the doctrine that if one's population were exposed to nuclear attack from one's enemy one would not dare to start a nuclear war.

The five-year interim agreement on offensive weapons allowed the Soviet Union to build up its ICBM force to 1,618 while the United States would keep its existing level of 1,054. The Soviets were allowed 950 submarine-launched ballistic missiles (SLBMs) and 62 submarines, while the United States was confined to 710 SLBMs and 44 submarines. Important weapon systems left out of the agreement—bombers, land mobile ICBMs, forward-based forces of less than intercontinental range, and multiple warheads—were to be the subject of the more comprehensive negotiations that were supposed to produce a completed treaty by October 1977.[12]

The allowance of a Soviet numerical advantage in ICBMs and SLBMs—though it attracted criticism from some quarters—was not yet of serious concern to the U.S. Defense Department, for in the items not covered by the agreement the United States was well ahead of the Soviets. U.S. defense hardliners allowed Kissinger and Nixon to have their way with a minimum of bureaucratic or congressional opposition to the agreements they brought home from Moscow. The hardliners deferred to Nixon's *political* judgments that the dramatic breakthrough in arms control was the centerpiece of the 1972 détente he had constructed with Brezhnev in Moscow and that his spectacular summit success was his best counter to "leftist" attacks on him for not yet having achieved a Vietnam peace. But the military preparedness coalition in Congress and the administration was determined to make the subsequent SALT negotiations more responsive to their interpretations of sufficiency. Senator Henry Jackson formulated a Senate Resolution which the administration accepted, insisting that in any future strategic weapons agreements with the USSR the United States not accept provisions, such as those in SALT I, that would leave the United States with numerical inferiority.

Kissinger's achievement in satisfying Nixon's political need for a dramatic démarche in U.S.–Soviet relations was made possible by his ability to cater to Brezhnev's analogous political needs, and to make these even more intense by the acceleration of détente diplomacy with the U.S.–China rapprochement.[13]

The temporarily suppressed contradictions—in the administration's sufficiency concept and in the Soviets' analogous dilemma of simultaneously agreeing to stabilize the arms race while continuing to deploy strategic forces with impressive war-fighting characteristics—were bound to surface again even before the ink was dry on the SALT I agreements.

In the summer of 1972, the Defense Department asked Congress to provide funds for the development of strategic warheads with "hard-target kill capabilities," and programs were accelerated for installing accurate MIRVs on U.S. ICBMs and submarine launched strategic missiles.[14]

In 1973 and 1974, under the new Secretary of Defense, James Schlesinger, the Pentagon further lifted the secrecy lid from its force planning premises. In a series of candid news conferences, Schlesinger revealed the administration's intention to acquire "precision instruments that would be used in a limited counterforce role" and, in fact, that it was refining its strategic targeting doctrine to give the President a "broader range of options." In addition, the administration was prepared, on the basis of its ongoing research and development programs, to balance any Soviet attempt to obtain a major counterforce option ("We cannot permit the other side to have a relatively credible counterforce capability if we lack the same").[15] Schlesinger's annual defense posture statement to Congress for fiscal year 1975 provided a carefully worded justification for the renewed emphasis on counterforce options:

> To enhance deterrence, we may want . . . a more efficient hardtarget kill capability than we now possess: both to threaten specialized sets of targets (possibly of concern to allies) with a greater economy of force, and to make it clear to a potential enemy that he cannot proceed with impunity to jeopardize our own system of hard targets. . . .
> To stress changes in targeting doctrine and new options does not mean radical departures from past practice. Nor does it imply any

possibility of acquiring a first strike disarming capability. As I have repeatedly stated, both the United States and the Soviet Union now have and will continue to have large, invulnerable second strike forces. . . .

We would be quite content if both the United States and the Soviet Union avoided the acquisition of major counterforce capabilities. But we are troubled by Soviet weapons momentum, and we simply cannot ignore the prospect of growing disparity between the two major nuclear powers. We do not propose to let an opponent threaten a major component of our forces without being able to pose a comparable threat. We do not propose to let an enemy put us in a position where we are left with no more than a capability to hold his cities hostage after the first phase of a nuclear conflict. And certainly we do not propose to see an enemy threaten one or more of our allies with his nuclear capabilities in the expectation that we would lack the flexibility and resolve to strike back at his assets.[16]

The main benchmarks previously outlined by President Nixon and Secretary Laird for establishing a sufficient U.S. strategic posture were thus elaborated by Schlesinger. However, particular stress was now accorded to "essential equivalence" with the Soviet Union in all the basic force characteristics ("throw-weight, accuracy, yield-to-weight ratios, reliability and other such factors") for reasons of military effectiveness *and* political appearances. The requirement was for "a range and magnitude of capabilities such that everyone—friend, foe, and domestic audiences alike—will perceive that we are the equal of our strongest competitors."[17] This meant that even though the Soviets might be exercising bad strategic logic in building forces that could destroy a large portion of the U.S. land-based ICBMs (bad logic in that the Soviet Union could still be destroyed by U.S. submarine-launched missiles and bombers), the United States—to preserve the appearance of symmetry—should also build such a counterforce capability.

Soviet defense programs were even more blatantly at cross-purposes with mutual strategic arms limitation. Consistent with the letter but not the spirit of the 1972 Moscow accords, the Russians continued to deploy heavy-payload ICBMs with substantial counterforce potential, and their military doctrine stressed the requirements of fighting and prevailing in a strategic war, more than deterrence. Evidence of continued Soviet reliance on heavy counterforce capabilities spurred U.S. defense planners to go ahead with new systems as a "hedge" against Soviet attempts to achieve strategic dominance. The major consequences were a full-speed-ahead program of retrofitting U.S. missiles with MIRV warheads, efforts to enhance the accuracy of all U.S. strategic systems (including submarine-launched missiles), and "next generation" bomber programs (the B-1 bomber and long-range cruise missiles for the modernized bomber force).

Kissinger and others who hoped to translate the 1972 interim agreement on offensive systems into a solid treaty by its expiration date of October 1977 were dismayed at the continued "qualitative" technological race proceeding on both sides. Not only was that race making a mockery of the quantitative limits agreed to in SALT I, but it was virtually precluding reliable verification of these or future limits. Kissinger's anxiety to put a cap on the accelerating competition before it was too late was reflected in his complaint at a Moscow press conference in connection with Nixon's 1974 visit that "both sides have to convince their military establishments of the benefits of restraint."[18]

The Secretary of State hastily arranged for Brezhnev and Ford to commit themselves, at their 1974 Vladivostok meeting, to negotiating a treaty that would at least freeze their arsenals at a specified number of strategic missile launchers (2,400 for each side), of which only a subset (1,320) could be MIRVed. Within the overall ceiling of 2,400, each side could deploy its own preferred mix of ICBMs, submarine-launched ballistic missiles, or bombers; and there was no specified limit on missile throw-weight.[19] The Vladivostok accord was a political holding action at the top to keep the objective of a mutual-deterrence treaty from being totally subverted by the combined pressures of technology and military doctrine, which, in the United States as well as in the Soviet Union, were tending more and more toward legitimate strategic counterforce and other war-fighting capabilities. When it came down to attempts to convert the Vladivostok principles into a stable and verifiable treaty, however, the military experts on both sides—even those who were dedicated to arms control—continued to be baffled by the increasing difficulty of distinguishing offensive from defensive deployments, strategic from tactical weapons, nuclear from conventional munitions, single from multiple warheads; and by the virtual impossibility of determining (in advance of its actually being used) whether a given weapon had a city or a missile complex as its primary target.

Kissinger's skepticism about the stability over time of any technical limitations on military hardware led him to concentrate more on the symbolic benefits of negotiating constructively with the Russions in the SALT arena than on the presumed military effects of any agreements that might be concluded. And his doubts that close attention to the military balance itself would be sufficient for the purpose of preventing the Russians from using military coercion against U.S. interests reinforced this belief in the necessity of nonmilitary levers on Soviet behavior. The China connection and the economic aspects of détente diplomacy were supposed to compensate for the shortfalls in military containment.

The China Angle

The Nixon–Kissinger construction of a new relationship with China preceded and gave major impetus to the rapid elaboration of the U.S.–Soviet détente relationship in the early 1970s. The China connection, conceived of primarily as a means of pressuring the Kremlin to be more accommodating to U.S. demands, was also designed to serve other objectives of the administration: an early end to the Vietnam war; a reduction in overseas deployment of American troops; a dismantling of military commitments to Asian regimes that might be unstable or reckless; and simply the need to do something dramatic to convince the American public and international audiences that the government, under Nixon's leadership, did have the capacity to act impressively on the world stage. The new China policy, not incidentally, also could give concrete substance to Kissinger's vague concept of an emerging multipolar world.

However much administration spokesmen might publicly deny that gaining leverage on the Soviet Union was the central purpose of the China connection, this geopolitical *result* of the new triangular relationship was undeniable, and was never really denied. But Nixon and Kissinger apparently calculated that the leverage would be just as great if it was kept implicit, and that the Soviets might not have been able to bring themselves to be accommodating toward the United States in various fields if it looked to the world as if they were negotiating under coercive pressure.

As Washington and Peking drew toward each other across the hypotenuse of the triangle from 1969 to 1972, the theatrics of the démarche began to eclipse the geopolitics, but the former in no way undermined the latter. The show business staging of the Nixon visit seemed only to convince the Russians of the need to stage a more impressive summit spectacular of their own.

Historians will long debate whether this turn in U.S.–China policy was mainly the brainchild of Nixon or of Kissinger (not to mention Mao Tse-tung and Chou En-lai).[20] A resolution of this controversy matters little for the present analysis. More important is the fact that both men came to believe by early 1969 that a movement toward normalizing relations with Peking might now mesh with Chinese calculations and significantly reinforce the Soviets' incentive to explore their own common interests with the United States.

China experts in and out of the government had been picking up signs during the late 1960s that Mao and Chou might be reading the tea leaves similarly. The Chinese condemned the Soviet invasion of Czechoslovakia in August 1968, and especially the doctrine of "limited sovereignty" of countries in the socialist camp by which the Soviets justified their invasion. Tension was heightening along the Sino-Soviet border in the aftermath of Czechoslovakia. In November 1968 the Chinese Foreign Ministry proposed a convening of the Sino-American ambassadorial talks in Warsaw, which had been suspended since January.[21]

The Nixon administration, while indicating its willingness to resume the heretofore sterile exchanges in Warsaw, was searching for fresh ways to convince the Chinese that the White House might be open to an exploration of some fundamental improvements in the relationship. Early in 1969 Nixon began to hint strongly through French, Rumanian, and Pakistani intermediaries that he would like to visit China.[22] Meanwhile, an informal coalition of liberal members of Congress and China experts— perhaps sensing that the administration was exploring a shift in policy—tried to create public support for normalizing relations with the communist regime. Senator Edward Kennedy, speaking on March 20, 1969, to a conference sponsored by the National Committee on United States–China Relations, urged that new initiatives be taken by the Nixon administration, such as the elimination of U.S. military bases in Taiwan and an offer to reestablish consular offices in the People's Republic. (The conference, chaired by former U.S. Ambassador to Japan Edwin O. Reischauer, took place two weeks after the outbreak of military conflict between Soviet and Chinese forces over a disputed island on the Ussuri River. China experts at the conference speculated that this development might provide an opportunity for a breakthrough in U.S.–China relations.)[23]

Starting in the summer of 1969, the Department of State began to announce various unilateral gestures of reconciliation. In July many travel and trade restrictions that had been applied to China since 1950 were relaxed. Americans traveling abroad would be permitted to bring back $100 worth of items produced in the People's Republic. Congressmen, journalists, teachers, scholars, university students, physicians, and Red Cross representatives would automatically be cleared by the Department for travel to China.[24] These moves were an effort to "relax tensions and facilitate the development of peaceful contacts," explained State Department spokesmen. These particular actions were chosen because they did not require Chinese reciprocation.

The premises underlying these gestures were partially revealed in an address on September 5, 1969, by Under Secretary
of State Elliot L. Richardson at the annual meeting of the American Political Science Association. "We do not seek to exploit for
our own advantage the hostility between the Soviet Union and
the People's Republic," said Richardson, deliberately injecting
the name of the Maoist government, in contrast to the previous
policy of only using the terms *Communist China* or *Mainland
China.*

> Ideological differences between the two Communist giants are
> not our affair. We could not fail to be deeply concerned, however,
> with an escalation of this quarrel into a massive breach of interna-
> tional peace and security. Our national security would in the long
> run be prejudiced by associating ourselves with either side against
> the other. Each is highly sensitive about American efforts to im-
> prove relations with the other. We intend, nevertheless, to pursue
> a long-term course of progressively developing better relations
> with both. We are not going to let Communist Chinese invective
> deter us from seeking agreements with the Soviet Union where
> those are in our interest. Conversely, we are not going to let Soviet
> apprehensions prevent us from attempting to bring Communist
> China out of its angry, alienated shell.[25]

Over the next year the administration continued to signal its
intent to put U.S.–Chinese relations on a new basis: In November 1969, U.S. naval patrols in the Taiwan Strait (deployed by
Truman at the start of the Korean War) were terminated, removing the most visible symbol of U.S. support for the nationalist
Chinese exiles. In December, the U.S. government partially
lifted the embargo on trade by foreign subsidiaries of U.S. firms
between China and third countries, again stating that the move
was "strictly unilateral." In January 1970, the U.S. and Chinese
ambassadors to Poland resumed their suspended talks in Warsaw and explored in a preliminary way the possibility of exchange visits by journalists, students, and scientists. On February 18, in the first of his four annual "State of the World"
messages to Congress, President Nixon, reiterating the theme
that "the Chinese are a great and vital people who should not

remain isolated from the international community," revealed
that it was administration policy to "attempt to define a new
relationship" for the future. "We have avoided dramatic gestures which might invite dramatic rebuffs," explained the President. "We have taken specific steps that did not require Chinese
agreements but which underlined our willingness to have a
more normal and constructive relationship."[26] Two days later, at
the ambassadorial talks in Warsaw, both sides discussed the possibility of moving the talks to Peking, and the Chinese hinted
that they would welcome a high-ranking official to head the U.S.
delegation.[27] This delicate courtship was set back somewhat during the spring and summer of 1970 as U.S. troops invaded Cambodia, while in China a struggle was played out between the Lin
Piao faction, which favored a hard line toward Washington as
well as Moscow, and the Chou En-lai faction, which favored a
moderate policy at home and abroad, including better relations
with the United States in order to put pressure on the Soviets.

Early in the fall of 1970 the atmosphere was suddenly alive with
possibility. Mao evidently had thrown his weight decisively behind Chou and seemed to be sending his own signals to Washington that a new era in Sino-American relations might now be
appropriate. Official Washington attached significance to Mao's
having asked the prominent American chronicler of the Chinese
communist revolution, Edgar Snow, to join him on the reviewing
stand for the National Day celebrations on October 1. Nixon and
Kissinger, sensing that the time was ripe, intensified their efforts
to communicate with the Chinese leaders via the Rumanians and
Pakistanis. Secret notes, presumably dealing with the possibility
of a high-level U.S. visit to China, were carried back and forth
through the winter months, except for a six-week hiatus in February and early March surrounding the invasion of Laos by South
Vietnamese troops with U.S. air support.[28]

Nixon and Kissinger used all available diplomatic channels to
reassure Mao that the Laos operation was not meant to threaten
China in any way. And in the second annual State of the World
Address to Congress the President reiterated his objective of
drawing China into "a serious dialog." He invited the "People's

Republic of China to explore the path of normalization of its relations with its neighbors and the world, including our own country." During the coming year, promised the President, "I will carefully examine what further steps we might take to create broader opportunities for contacts between the Chinese and American peoples, and how we might remove needless obstacles to the realization of these opportunities. We hope for, but will not be deterred by, a lack of reciprocity." This effort, the President explained, was part of the main foreign policy approach of his administration: "to create a balanced international structure in which all nations have a stake. We believe that such a structure should provide full scope for the influence to which China's achievements entitle it."[29]

The breakthrough occurred early in the spring of 1971 (the chroniclers of the period are not precise as to the date), when the Pakistani ambassador to the United States delivered a handwritten note from Peking, with no signature, inviting an "American envoy" to come to China for high-level talks. The note suggested either Kissinger or Secretary of State Rogers.[30] The invitation and the decision to send Kissinger to Peking were closely held secrets. The public was allowed the fantasy that the U.S. ping pong team, touring China in April 1971 at the sudden invitation of Chou En-lai, was the vehicle through which the inscrutable Chinese were making known to the White House their willingness to explore an improvement in relations. While the Ping-Pong team was still in China, Nixon announced further relaxation of the twenty-year embargo on trade with the People's Republic. A Chinese Ping-Pong team was, of course, invited to tour the United States. And at the end of April Nixon began to hint unsubtly to journalists and foreign diplomats that he himself would like to be invited to visit China.

The Chinese cooperated in keeping under wraps Kissinger's secret July 1971 mission to Peking to arrange for the Nixon visit, so that the President himself could make a surprise announcement of the dramatic development after the fact. Nixon and Kissinger apparently felt they needed a *fait accompli* to overcome opposition to such a move from the Taiwan government and its

U.S. supporters. In the playing out of this surprise, they knew they would cause anxiety in the Kremlin. The strategem also shocked and angered the Japanese and other allied governments, but the affronts to established friends were presumed to be ultimately retrievable costs well worth the benefits of the new shift in global power relationships.

It was more than mere coincidence that Nixon's July 15 announcement that he would visit China was followed by his revelation in an August 4 press conference that he and the Soviet leaders had agreed that there should be a U.S.–Soviet summit meeting when there was something substantive to discuss that could not be handled in other channels. Nixon indicated that ongoing discussions with the Soviets were making progress in a number of fields—Berlin, SALT, the Mideast—and added pointedly that "if the time comes, as it may come, and both sides realize this, then the final breakthrough in any one of these areas can take place only at the highest level, and then there will be a meeting. But as far as the timing of the meeting before the visit to Peking, that would not be an appropriate thing to do.[31]

The Russians got the message and picked up on the cue. The early fall of 1971 was a particularly congenial season at various U.S.–Soviet negotiating tables. Agreements were reached on procedures for preventing nuclear accidents and on improving the emergency "hot line" between Washington and Moscow. And most significant, a preliminary accord was reached on the outlines of a Berlin settlement. President Nixon announced on October 12 that he had accepted Chairman Brezhnev's invitation to visit Moscow in May. Kissinger again traveled to Peking at the end of October—this time in the full glare of news media—to firm up plans for Nixon to visit China in February.

It was more than coincidental that Kissinger would be in Peking while the issue of China's representation in the United Nations was brought to a vote in New York. The latest U.S. position—ending twenty years of opposition to the Peking government's membership in the world organization, but still refusing to countenance the expulsion of Taiwan—was announced by Secretary of State Rogers on August 2 and stoutly defended in UN

debates by Ambassador George Bush in the face of clear indications that the majority would take an unequivocal pro-Peking
stand. In the key resolution on October 25, the General Assembly decided (by a vote of 76 to 35, with 17 abstentions) to recognize the representatives of the People's Republic as "the only legitimate representatives of China" and to "expell forthwith the
representatives of Chiang Kai-shek from the place which they
unlawfully occupy at the United Nations and in all the organizations affiliated with it." The White House immediately issued a
statement accepting the will of the majority but regretting the
expulsion of Taiwan.

The year 1972 was to be, in effect, the Year of the Triangle: the
year of maximum exploitation by the Nixon administration of its
new China connection to pressure the Kremlin into accommoda-
tionist positions on SALT, European security issues, and the conflict in Southeast Asia; the year of maximum exploitation of the
growing U.S.–Soviet détente to induce the Chinese to be patient
with the United States for continuing to recognize the government of Taiwan and for its slow-paced disengagement from
Southeast Asia; and the year of maximum exploitation of Nixon's
popularity in both Moscow and Peking to induce the North Vietnamese to seriously negotiate an Indochina peace agreement
with the United States. Not incidentally, the simultaneity of all
this with the U.S. presidential election campaign was fortuitous,
and was also exploited to the hilt.

Uncertain of the strength of the incentives of either Moscow
or Peking to put good relations with the United States ahead of
its other international and domestic objectives, the White House
was anxious not to appear too blatant in playing on the Machia-
vellian triangle. Repeatedly, in statements preceding and following the President's trip to China, Nixon and Kissinger insisted
that "our policy is not aimed against Moscow. The United States
and the USSR have issues of paramount importance to resolve;
it would be costly indeed to impair progress on these through
new antagonisms." To attempt to use the opening to Peking "to
exploit Sino-Soviet tensions . . . would be self-defeating and
dangerous."[32]

The Chinese were more candid with respect to their own reasons for seeking a rapprochement with the United States. The official Peking journal *Hungchi* reprinted a 1940 article by Mao propounding the wisdom of "uniting with forces that can be united while isolating and hitting the most obdurate enemies."[33]

The Americans were successful, however, in keeping direct anti-Soviet statements out of the communiqué issued by President Nixon and Premier Chou En-lai in Shanghai at the conclusion of the Nixon visit. In the language of the communiqué, "The two sides state that . . . neither should seek hegemony in the Asia–Pacific region and each is opposed to efforts by any other country or group of countries to establish such hegemony." And, in a stroke of studied ambiguity, "Both sides are of the view that it would be against the interest of the peoples of the world for any major country to collude with another against other countries, or for major countries to divide up the world into spheres of interest."[34]

Even in the parts of the communiqué reserved for unilateral statements by each side, the Chinese, deferring to U.S. sensitivities, threw their barbs at the Russians in clever general formulations that could be applied to either the Americans or the Russians. Thus,

> The Chinese side stated: Wherever there is oppression, there is resistance. Countries want independence, nations want liberation and the people want revolution—this has become the irresistible trend of history. All nations, big or small, should be equal; big nations should not bully the weak. China will never be a superpower and it opposes hegemony and power politics of any kind. The Chinese side stated that it firmly supports the struggles of all the oppressed people and nations for freedom and liberation and that the people of all countries have a right to choose their social systems according to their own wishes and the right to safeguard the independence, sovereignty and territorial integrity of their own countries and oppose foreign aggression, interference, control and subversion. All foreign troops should be withdrawn to their own countries.[35]

For the most sensitive issue between the United States and China—the problem of Taiwan—the device of including two separate statements in the communiqué was indispensable. The Chinese reaffirmed their longstanding position that "Taiwan is a province of China . . . ; the liberation of Taiwan is China's internal affair in which no other country has a right to interfere; and all U.S. forces and military installations must be withdrawn from Taiwan." The Americans attempted to finesse the issue as much as they could, declaring, in one of the most carefully crafted statements in the annals of diplomacy, that

> the United States acknowledges that all Chinese on either side of the Taiwan Strait maintain there is but one China and that Taiwan is a part of China. The United States Government does not challenge that position. It reaffirms its interest in a peaceful settlement of the Taiwan question by the Chinese themselves. With this prospect in mind, it affirms the ultimate objective of the withdrawal of all U.S. forces from Taiwan. In the meantime, it will progressively reduce its forces and military installations on Taiwan as the tension in the area diminishes."[36]

By granting the legitimacy of even this thin line of disagreement, however, Mao and Chou had made a substantial concession in the service of the higher goal they shared with Nixon and Kissinger of normalizing U.S.–China relations in order to gain new leverage on the Russians.

The most candid public exposition by a U.S. official of the connection between U.S. policies toward the Soviet Union and U.S. policies toward China was made by Winston Lord, director of the State Department's Policy Planning Staff (and Kissinger's closest aide on China policy). In a statement to a House subcommittee in March 1976, later published in a Department of State *Bulletin* under the title "The Triangular Relationship of the United States, the USSR, and the People's Republic of China," Lord put "improved prospects for global equilibrium" at the top of the list of benefits accruing to the United States from positive relations with China, and "a hedge against Soviet diplomatic and military pressures" as first among the advantages to be derived by the Chinese.

Lord's testimony reiterated the standard official position that an attempt by the United States to manipulate the Sino-Soviet rivalry, to meddle in it, or to take sides would be dangerous and self-defeating. "At the same time," he observed, "in a triangular relationship it is undeniably advantageous for us to have better relations with each of the other two actors than they have with one another." The United States has no desire to see the Sino-Soviet rivalry escalate into military conflict, said Lord, but "neither can we genuinely wish to see the two major communist powers locked once again in close alliance." In a meticulously formulated qualification, he granted that "a limited thaw in Sino-Soviet relations, however, would not automatically redound to our disadvantage, provided it was not based on shared opposition to the United States." An almost humorous understatement summed up the essence of the approach: "The record to date suggests that improvement in our ties with one does not harm our ties with the other."[37]

Kissinger himself would insist on this public rationale for the China rapprochement through the last days of his tenure as Secretary of State (and it would be surprising if he went beyond it in his memoirs). In an interview with the *New York Times* on the eve of Jimmy Carter's inauguration, he once again stressed that "it is a mistake to define the Sino-Soviet relationship in terms of our exploiting their differences . . . We didn't create them, we can't exploit them." But he went on, in a characteristic circumlocution, to place the triangular relationship at the center of his basic geopolitical strategy:

> I believe it is important that the People's Republic of China continue to perceive us as interested in maintaining a world equilibrium. If they feel we have lost our interest in it or our comprehension of it, or our willingness to preserve it, then they will draw the inevitable conclusion, which will be to make whatever accommodation they can get [with the Soviet Union], or they will try to find some other means of protection, such as organizing the third world against both of us.[38]

The Commercial Lever

The Nixon–Kissinger attempt to gain economic leverage on the Soviet Union's international behavior in order to compensate for the insufficiency of military containment was a throwback to a strategy proposed to President Truman by Averell Harriman in 1945. Harriman, then ambassador to Moscow, urged the new President to face down the Russians where they behaved antagonistically to U.S. interests. The United States could be tough toward the Soviets without running serious risks, counseled Harriman, since this country was the only source of economic help for their postwar reconstruction. In Truman's words, "The Russians needed us more than we needed them." The early postwar strategy of economic leverage was soon discarded, however. Stalin's paranoia about Western motives and his evident willingness to pay the price of Western animosity rather than forgo the incorporation of Eastern Europe into the Soviet sphere of control convinced Truman and his advisers that the West must rely almost entirely on military power to contain the Russians.[39]

During the Kennedy and Johnson administrations, policy makers flirted with the idea of affecting Soviet behavior through commerce. The hope was to eventually stimulate consumer demands that would make it more difficult for the Kremlin to sustain high military budgets. Some champions of greater East–West commercial intercourse thought it might also encourage the Soviets to experiment with economic liberalization measures. It was not unreasonable to believe, said the Assistant Secretary of State for Economic Affairs, Anthony Solomon, "that small steps toward more normal intercourse might over the long term have a cumulative beneficial effect in reducing the aggressive thrust of Soviet policy."[40] Presidents Kennedy and Johnson each asked Congress to approve the sale of wheat to the Soviet Union as a step toward opening up limited commercial relations in other sectors. But such moves were tentative and peripheral to the main thrust of U.S. policy until the Nixon–Kissinger years.

It was not until well into the third year of the Nixon administration that the attempt to construct a commercial relationship between the two superpowers became an integral part of U.S. policy. But as with the change in policy toward China, the premises of this policy shift were only partly revealed to the public. Signs that the grounds of U.S. policy on East–West trade were being altered were picked up in the fall of 1971 by American firms, which suddenly began to experience success in obtaining previously denied licenses to export their products to the Soviet Union. The coincidence of the export license liberalization with the firming up of plans for Nixon to visit China and collateral progress toward a Nixon–Brezhnev summit was hardly accidental.

In the fall of 1971, the positive side of Kissinger's linkage strategy was in full swing. The Russians, woefully short of wheat for the coming winter as a result of a dismal harvest, were allowed to purchase $1 billion of American surplus food grains. The State Department indicated its readiness to reduce various discriminatory shipping regulations on Soviet vessels visiting U.S. ports. The Secretary of Commerce took a highly publicized trip to the Soviet Union surrounded by background stories from government ministries in both countries on the possibilities of pushing U.S.–Soviet trade to the $5 billion-a-year level by the mid 1970s. Appetites on both sides were whetted with visions of cooperative efforts to develop the oil, gas, and hard mineral riches of Siberia. By the spring of 1972, progress on numerous bilateral commercial negotiations between subordinate levels of the governments was sufficiently advanced for the subject of a general U.S.–Soviet commercial rapprochement to be included as a major item on the agenda for the May summit meeting. Indeed, the Russians appeared to be more enthusiastic about normalizing economic relations than about any other aspect of détente, and this probably was the reason that they refrained from canceling the 1972 summit in the face of highly coercive U.S. actions against North Vietnam in the spring of 1972 (including the mining of Haiphong harbor, which, not incidentally, interfered with Soviet shipping).

The "basic principles" signed by President Nixon and General Secretary Brezhnev on May 29, 1972, affirmed that "The U.S.A. and the U.S.S.R. regard commercial and economic ties as an important and necessary element in the strengthening of their bilateral relations and will thus actively promote the growth of such ties. They will facilitate cooperation between the relevant

organizations and enterprises of the two countries and the conclusion of appropriate agreements and contracts, including long-
term ones."[41] By the end of the year, the accomplishments
under this accord included an agreement by the Russians to pay
back $722 million on their wartime Lend-Lease debt by the year
2001, in return for which President Nixon would now authorize
the Export-Import Bank to extend credits and guarantees for the
sale of goods to the Soviet Union; a commitment by the Nixon
administration to seek congressional extension of most-favored-
nation tariff rates to the Soviet Union; the delivery of 440 million
bushels of wheat to the Soviet Union; a maritime agreement
opening 40 ports in each nation to the other's shipping; provision for the United States to set up government-sponsored and
commercial offices in Moscow to facilitate the work of U.S. businessmen seeking contracts, and similar provisions for the Russians in Washington; and the establishment of a Joint U.S.–
Soviet Commercial Commission charged with developing and
guiding the elaboration of additional arrangements to encourage
U.S.–Soviet commerce.

The new policy rested on a number of publicly stated premises, but also on some premises that remained unarticulated,
apparently for fear of embarrassing the Kremlin. The openly articulated premises underlying the expansion of U.S.–Soviet commerce were the following:

> —Recent progress on basic political issues (the framework
> and terms for SALT, and the status of Berlin) made it possi-
> ble to initiate discussions on a wide range of projects for
> bilateral cooperation in nonpolitical fields.
> —As cooperation in nonpolitical fields widened and
> deepened, they would reinforce the trend toward more
> constructive political relations.
> —Bilateral economic arrangements, at first mainly involving
> trade, could later be broadened to include longer-term
> cooperative ventures that would "establish an interdepen-
> dence between our economies which provides a continuing
> incentive to maintain a constructive relationship."

—As the nonpolitical relationships continued to expand, side by side with continuing progress on arms control and other political issues, there would be created on each side "a vested interest in restraint and in the preservation of peace."[42]

The most elaborate statement of the key premise that a growing web of economic arrangements could reduce political hostility between the United States and the Soviet Union was contained in a report to the President by Secretary of Commerce Peter Peterson, released to the public in August 1972:

> Closer economic ties bear both cause and effect relationships to relaxation of political tension. Improvement in political relationships is a prerequisite for improved economic relationships, but, once in place, economic ties create a community of interest which in turn improves the environment for further progress on the political side.
>
> Once set in motion, the cause-and-effect process can portend a downward spiral in political tension, a mutually beneficial economic foundation of the new relationship and tangible increases in the welfare and safety of the peoples of both countries. . . .
>
> Our purpose is . . . to build in both countries a vested economic interest in the maintenance of an harmonious and enduring relationship. A nation's security is affected not only by its adversary's military capabilities but by the price which attends the use of those capabilities. If we can create a situation in which the use of military force would jeopardize a mutually profitable relationship, I think it can be argued that our security will have been enhanced.[43]

One who read between the lines of the public rationale and had occasion to discuss with U.S. policymakers their considerations at the time could ascertain a set of tougher assumptions underlying the effort to open up commerce with the Soviet Union, namely:

—The Kremlin leadership recognized that a continued modernization of the USSR would require a substantial shift of resources into many of the high technology, largely civilian areas that until recently had been low priority in comparison with military needs.

—But Brezhnev and his comrades also realized that, in order to close the modernization gap in the civilian economy and simultaneously maintain military parity with the United States, the Soviet Union would require substantial inputs from the West, especially in the fields of information technology and electronics.

—The needed Western economic and technological inputs could not be purchased without large credits from the United States and other advanced industrial countries and an improvement in the Soviet Union's export potential.

—Finally, the Russian leaders had come to believe, despite the Leninist dictum that capitalists would sell the hangman the rope to be used in their own executions, that only a fully credible Soviet policy of peaceful coexistence would stimulate the noncommunist countries to extend sufficient credits, to liberalize their strategic lists, and otherwise let down their political barriers to East–West commerce.

—In short, the Soviet Union's *economic* need to open up commerce with the industrial countries was greater than the latter's need for commerce with the communist countries; therefore, if the United States and its allies wisely bargained with the Soviet Union from this basic position of economic strength, the Russians, if not openly backed into a corner, might be willing to pay a *political* price for an expansion of East–West commerce.

Such, undoubtedly, were the unvarnished assumptions beneath the Kissinger gloss that "we have approached the question of economic relations with deliberation and circumspection and as an act of policy not primarily of commercial opportunity."[44] Apparently, the main political price Nixon and Kissinger wanted the Russians to pay was to stop aiding the North Vietnamese war effort in Indochina and to bring pressure on Hanoi to negotiate seriously with the United States to wind down the war.

The U.S. mining of Haiphong harbor took place just two weeks before President Nixon was due in Moscow for his first summit conference with Secretary Brezhnev. The Soviet Minister of Foreign Trade was in the United States at the time for an intense round of presummit commercial negotiations with Secretary of Commerce Peterson and other officials whose results were to be unveiled with much fanfare in Moscow. Nixon and Kissinger had doubts that the Moscow summit would be allowed to proceed on schedule, but they continued to remind the Russians of what was at stake. Kissinger's May 9 briefing to newsmen on the Haiphong mining included a pointed reference to the negotiations in progress with the Soviet Union: "We are on the verge of a new relationship in which, on both sides, whenever there is a danger of crisis, there will be enough people who have a commitment to constructive programs so that they could exercise restraining influences."[45]

During the next few years, when the President or Kissinger publicly observed that détente itself was in jeopardy as a result of Soviet actions—for example, the threat to land Soviet paratroops in the Middle East in 1973 or the Soviet transport of Cuban forces to Angola—they clearly meant to play upon the Kremlin's presumed high motivation for commercial relations with the West. They did not, however, believe that the Kremlin's motivation for commercial relations was so high that U.S. credits and trading privileges could be used as a lever to directly induce changes *within* the Soviet system. This was their objection to the Jackson-Vanik Amendment to the Trade Reform Act of 1974, which sought to deny most-favored-nation trading status and credits to the Soviet Union if the Kremlin did not substantially remove restrictions on Jewish emigration. The administration claimed to be effectively representing the attitudes of the American people toward the denial of human rights in the USSR, but it regarded the Jackson-Vanik Amendment and the Stevenson Amendment (setting a $300 million limit on Export-Import Bank credits to the Soviet Union) as at best unhelpful and at worst likely to revive the bitterness of the cold war. "We have accomplished much," claimed Kissinger in 1974, "but we cannot demand that the Soviet Union, in effect, suddenly reverse five decades of Soviet, and centuries of Russian, history."[46]

The administration did, however, cooperate with the West Europeans in linking East–West economic cooperation to "basket three" human rights issues at the Helsinki Conference on Security and Cooperation in Europe. The Russians probably found it tolerable to go along with such linkage since the Helsinki language was ambiguous and not explicitly directed at them, nor did the accords themselves contain any sanctions for noncompliance. From the standpoint of the administration, overuse or premature application of economic sanctions (denial of credits and trade) was in any case undesirable, for it would reduce the leverage the United States might obtain from ongoing arrangements.

On the other hand, the administration also belatedly came to the realization that, in the process of attempting to make the Soviet Union more dependent on the noncommunist world by removing political barriers to East–West trade, it may have, paradoxically, been creating some cumbersome interdependencies. This problem surfaced most clearly in the concession by both parties' 1976 presidential candidates to demands by U.S. agricultural interest groups that there be no further imposition of embargoes on grain shipments to the Soviet Union. The Ford administration's growing appreciation of the difficulty of operating a policy of economic leverage was reflected in the complaint by a high State Department official that "there has been a tendency in Western countries to let the legitimate quest for commercial advantage in Eastern markets overshadow the need to develop and pursue a purposeful strategy. This has tended to undercut the influences which the economic strength of the industrialized world could exert."[47]

All in all, Kissinger left office on January 20, 1977, with the non-military levers on the Soviet Union that were central to his grand strategy having become objects of growing skepticism in the U.S. policy community. His own doubts about their efficacy, if not supported by a domestic consensus, were reflected in his renewed emphasis in late 1976 (and in subsequent statements as a private citizen) on local balances of military power as essential for containing the Soviets.

3

☆☆ ☆AVOIDING HUMILIATION IN INDOCHINA

> Our defeat and humiliation in South Vietnam without question would promote recklessness in the councils of those great powers who have not yet abandoned their goals of world conquest.
>
> Richard Nixon in November 1969*

By the time Richard Nixon assumed the Presidency, few Americans still believed that communist domination of the Indochinese peninsula would pose an intolerable threat to U.S. security. The main question was no longer *whether* the United States should slough off responsibility for preventing the North Vietnamese and the Vietcong from taking over South Vietnam, but *how* to liquidate this costly commitment.

Like Lyndon Johnson at the end of his Presidency, the new President and his principal national security adviser believed the prestige of the United States still was heavily at stake in Vietnam; and they discerned a popular mandate that the United States exit from Vietnam "with honor." There were differences, however, between the administration and its critics, and even within the administration, over the ingredients of national honor.

To Nixon and Kissinger, as to Johnson, the nation's honor was bound up closely with its "credibility"—its reputation for keeping promises—and its refusal to be coerced by other nations. "The commitment of 500,000 Americans has settled the issue of the importance of Vietnam," wrote Kissinger in 1968. "For what

*"The Pursuit of Peace in Vietnam," *Department of State Bulletin,* no. 1587 (November 24, 1969), 61:438.

is involved now is confidence in American promises. However fashionable it is to ridicule the terms 'credibility' or 'prestige,' they are not empty phrases; other nations can gear their actions to ours only if they can count on our steadiness."[1]

But in view of many other Americans this country was being *dis*honored in Vietnam by its stubborn attempt to keep its promise to stop a communist takeover. An enlarging chorus of religious leaders, academics, students, media commentators, and politicians in both parties tried to convince the administration of its folly. It was dishonorable, they argued, for the United States to compel its young men to kill and be killed in a small, faraway country in the vain hope of helping a repressive and corrupt regime defeat the communists in a civil war. It was dishonorable for the United States to persist in trying to bomb North Vietnam into a submissive withdrawal of its forces in the face of clear evidence that the North Vietnamese were deeply and unequivocably commited to the "liberation" of the South.

According to various accounts, Nixon and Kissinger both recognized, even before taking office, that the honor of the United States was being sullied by its military involvement in Vietnam. They understood that the war was unwinnable and that the United States was being made to look foolish before the rest of the world as it wasted more and more of its substance in a country of minor strategic importance.[2] The trick was to withdraw from the war without having it appear that the United States was giving up. This policy had two essential features: "Vietnamization" and a negotiated settlement with Hanoi. The fighting itself was to be turned over to the South Vietnamese to continue on their own, not because the United States could no longer stomach being in the war but because Saigon had been strengthened sufficiently by U.S. help. Meanwhile, Hanoi would agree to pull its forces back into North Vietnam and to support political arrangements that would give the South Vietnamese communists (the National Liberation Front) a share in the governance of South Vietnam. The negotiating agenda and process, as outlined in Kissinger's January 1969 article in *Foreign Affairs*, would take place on two tracks: North Vietnam and the United

States to effect military disengagement, the National Liberation Front and the Thieu regime in Saigon to decide the political arrangement for South Vietnam.

As this became the Nixon administration's public posture, Hanoi presumably would see that what was being asked for was a "decent interval" to allow the United States to pull out with its honor intact, after which the North and South Vietnamese could settle the fate of their country without outside interference. Hanoi's maximum demand, of course, was an even larger capitulation by the United States and Saigon involving full withdrawal of U.S. forces, without a reciprocal pullback of the North Vietnamese, and the resignation of the Thieu government—prior to a cease-fire in South Vietnam and the start of processes to reconstitute a new government. But Kissinger apparently believed that Hanoi would understand Washington's need to avoid a humiliating exit and therefore could be persuaded to cooperate in choreographing an elaborate finale of mutual concessions.

Only a few days after Nixon's inauguration, the President and Kissinger moved to present their scheme directly to the North Vietnamese through Henry Cabot Lodge, their newly appointed head of the team negotiating with the North Vietnamese in Paris. The proposal Lodge carried to Paris was in essence the two-track process outlined in Kissinger's *Foreign Affairs* article, with the first step being a simultaneous *mutual* withdrawal of U.S. and North Vietnamese troops from South Vietnam—a change from the Johnson administration's position, which had held out for a withdrawal of North Vietnamese troops and a reduction of the level of violence in the South as the preconditions for U.S. troop withdrawal.[3]

Nixon and Kissinger were determined that the Paris negotiations should stop being a charade, and accordingly they pulled out all the stops so as to maximize the incentives operating on North Vietnam to come to the negotiating table with an equally serious intent to conclude a settlement. They set in motion a series of phased, unilateral reductions in U.S. ground forces in Vietnam, but simultaneously revealed a capability and will to bomb North Vietnam and North Vietnamese staging areas in

Cambodia and Laos with less squeamishness than the previous administration had shown. Meanwhile, they intensified pressure on Moscow and Peking to persuade Hanoi to negotiate an end to the war.

The administration pursued this multipronged strategy relentlessly for four years—continuing to make concessions in the U.S. negotiating position, gradually accelerating our unilateral troop withdrawals, applying larger doses of military coercion against North Vietnam, and attempting to thicken the links between Soviet and Chinese constructive influence on their North Vietnamese ally and U.S. responsiveness to Soviet or Chinese interests in other fields. With the signing of a mutually acceptable settlement in 1973, the strategy appeared to have worked, at least in the sense of providing an "honorable" cover for the U.S. military exit.

However, it took only two years for the cover itself to disintegrate completely. In the spring of 1975, with the Cambodian communists (the Khmer Rouge) marching on Phnom Penh and the North Vietnamese armies closing in on Saigon, President Ford and Secretary Kissinger struck one last pose of support for their now-abandoned allies in Indochina. Knowing full well that the majority in Congress, reflecting a broad popular consensus, had no intention of diverting further national resources to a lost cause, the administration nevertheless asked for a supplemental military aid package for the anticommunists in Cambodia and Vietnam. It was a transparent effort, at the last, to once again cast the blame for defeat on Congress in a desperate attempt to salvage the honor of the administration.

As the Vietcong raised their flag over Saigon and renamed it Ho Chi Minh City, the lack of any substantial popular interest in the outcome was, ironically, at least a partial vindication of the administration's strategy.

But this final denouement was a far cry from the Nixon–Kissinger script, which—more clearly in retrospect than during its unfolding—can be seen to have contained two fatal flaws: (1) the assumption that Hanoi would settle for anything less than a total victory over Saigon and (2) the assumption that the North

Vietnamese would perceive that Nixon and Kissinger, while sincerely determined to pull U.S. military forces out of Vietnam, could not be party to the total defeat of the anticommunist forces in Indochina. As it turned out, Hanoi's objectives were unequivocally total, and it remained unswerving in its conviction that the United States would give up even the ghost of a compromise settlement.

The dogged persistence of the belief that Hanoi's settling price was less than its repeated demands and that the positive and negative pressures on Hanoi would convince the communists that they had to compromise prolonged the agony and brutality of the U.S. involvement four years longer than Kissinger originally promised it would take him to end it. The costs of the delays would continue to haunt all those associated with the effort: more than 15,000 Americans killed and 53,000 wounded from 1969 to 1973, not to speak of the far greater losses by the Vietnamese on both sides.

Overestimation of Hanoi's susceptibility to coercion and positive inducements distorted the U.S. peace efforts at virtually every benchmark along the way to the communists' final victory. Distorted judgments were present in the basic approach of phasing in "Vietnamization" of the ground war while phasing out U.S. troops, in the graduated U.S. concessions to Hanoi's demands, in the dramatic escalations that followed in reaction to the communists' rejection or ignoring of these concessions, and even in the Paris Peace Accords themselves.

The administration's unfounded views about the North Vietnamese were paralleled by its overestimation of the humiliation the U.S. government would suffer in the eyes of the American public and other nations if it "precipitously" gave up fighting in Vietnam. By 1971 opinion polls revealed that a substantial majority of U.S. citizens wanted to end the war, even at the risk of an eventual communist takeover,[4] and most of the friends of the United States in Europe and Japan were embarrassed by their most powerful ally's irrational squandering of its human and material resources in a theater of secondary geopolitical significance.

Kissinger's attempt to dignify as a "tragedy" his and Nixon's prolongation of the bloodshed to gain an honorable peace in Indochina was transparent charlatanism. They had, primarily through their own rhetoric, backed themselves into a corner from which there was no escape except to admit that they were wrong. But such a noble course was evidently beyond these stubbornly proud men.

The Invasion of Cambodia: Nixon's "Seventh Crisis"

The invasion of Cambodia by U.S. troops on April 28, 1970, marked the end of the administration's ability to convince wide segments of the policy community that the White House really did have a workable "game plan" for ending the war. Clearly, Nixon and Kissinger, no less than their predecessors, had little control over the significant events and actors in Indochina and had lost whatever intellectual or conceptual control over the situation they might have started out with in 1969, not to speak of the emotional control required to implement a strategy of deliberate, cool military disengagement. Nixon called his own agonizing over the invasion decision his "seventh crisis."[5] Kissinger found himself the object of intense animosity on the part of former academic colleagues and members of his own staff, four of whom resigned.

From the point of view of Nixon and Kissinger, the opposition to the Cambodian invasion was a typical expression of the naiveté and spinelessness of the liberal eastern establishment. Cambodia's neutral status had already been systematically violated for more than a year by the belligerents on both sides: North Vietnamese soldiers had been using the Cambodian territory behind the South Vietnamese border to mass troops and supplies for their planned final march on Saigon, and U.S. B-52s had been bombarding these staging areas since March 1969 with the acquiescence of the Cambodian ruler, Prince Sihanouk. The bombing had been concealed from the American public and even from many national security officials in the administration. William Beecher, the Pentagon correspondent of the *New York Times,* broke the story in early May; however, it was not until after the spring 1972 invasion of Cambodia that the bombing was officially acknowledged.

Frustrated by the continuing refusal of Hanoi to discuss a mutual withdrawal of "foreign" forces from South Vietnam even as the United States began a good faith withdrawal of its own forces, and genuinely worried that the North Vietnamese might pounce on the South as soon as U.S. force levels got low enough, Nixon and Kissinger evidently felt by the spring of 1970 that they had no alternative but to break out of the pattern of weak signals they were transmitting to Hanoi.

Their opportunity came in March 1970 with the sudden right-wing coup in Phnom Penh that deposed Prince Sihanouk while he was out of the country. Marshal Lon Nol, the leader of the military coup, not only turned against the Cambodian communists but also attempted to force the North Vietnamese contingents out of his country. The North Vietnamese, no longer constrained to respect the independence of Cambodia, now openly and vigorously supported the Cambodian communists who were building up their forces around Phnom Penh in preparation for a countercoup. Lon Nol's desperate plea for U.S. help could not· be refused if the North Vietnamese were to be prevented from taking over Cambodia and completely outflanking South Vietnam. "If, when the chips are down," said Nixon, announcing the decision to attack the North Vietnamese sanctuaries in Cambodia,

> the world's most powerful nation, the United States of America, acts like a pitiful, helpless giant, the forces of totalitarianism and anarchy will threaten free nations and free institutions throughout the world. It is not our power but our will and character that is being tested tonight. If we fail to meet this challenge, all other nations will be on notice that despite its overwhelming power the United States, when a real crisis comes, will be found wanting.[6]

Although the foray into Cambodia, like most of the dramatic escalations ordered by Nixon, was designed primarily to shock

Hanoi into willingness to compromise, the official public explanations stressed a limited military objective. "This is not an invasion of Cambodia," insisted the President. "The areas in which these attacks will be launched are completely occupied and controlled by North Vietnamese forces. Our purpose is not to occupy the areas. Once enemy forces are driven out of these sanctuaries and once their military supplies are destroyed, we will withdraw."[7]

According to one of the Kissinger aides who resigned in protest over the Cambodia affair, the President authorized the operation even though he had been briefed by the Secretary of Defense three days before that the main North Vietnamese units were not really located in the areas to be attacked. The combined U.S.–South Vietnamese troops could achieve little more militarily than a temporary destruction of supply dumps and possibly a diversion of North Vietnamese forces, which were grouping elsewhere for an attack on the Cambodian capital.[8]

Two months later, on June 30, 1970, the President proclaimed the Cambodian operation a complete success and announced that all American troops had been withdrawn from Cambodia on schedule. He reeled off the indicators of enemy's material and human losses, with a curious, if not spurious, exactitude: "22,892 individual weapons . . . 2,509 big crew-served weapons. . . . More than 15 million rounds of ammunition. . . . 14 million pounds of rice. . . . 143,00 rockets. . . . Over 199,552 antiaircraft rounds, 5,482 mines, 62,022 grenades, and 83,000 pounds of explosives, including 1,002 satchel charges. . . . Over 435 vehicles . . . over 11,688 bunkers and other military structures . . . 11,349 men killed and about 2,328 captured and detainees."

The "deeper meaning" of these "impressive statistics," said Nixon, was as follows:

> We have eliminated an immediate threat to our forces and to the security of South Vietnam—and produced the prospect of fewer American casualties in the future.
> We have inflicted extensive casualties and very heavy losses in

material on the enemy—losses which can now be replaced only from the North during a monsoon season. . . .

We have ended the concept of Cambodian sanctuaries, immune from attack, upon which the enemy military had relied for five years.

We have dislocated supply lines and disrupted Hanoi's strategy in the Saigon area and the Mekong Delta. The enemy capacity to mount a major offensive in this vital populated region of the South has been greatly diminished.

We have effectively cut off the enemy from resupply by the sea. . . .

We have, for the time being, separated the Communist main-force units . . . from the guerillas in the southern part of Vietnam. This should provide a boost to pacification efforts.

We have guaranteed the continuance of our troop withdrawal program. . . .

We have bought time for the South Vietnamese to strengthen themselves against the enemy.

We have witnessed visible proof of the success of Vietnamization as the South Vietnamese performed with skill and valor and competence far beyond the expectation of our commanders or American advisers.[9]

President Nixon understandably chose not to refer to the fact that after the sixty-day U.S. incursion into Cambodia the communist forces occupied a larger portion of the country—about half of it. Nor did he choose to dwell on the ultimate political consequences of, in effect, conspiring with Hanoi to widen the battlefield irrevocably to include another of the three Indochinese countries.

Moreover, although the purpose of the operation was to shock Hanoi into facing up to the costs of continuing the war, it had the boomerang effect of finally shattering whatever confidence remained in the White House that the administration could revive popular faith in its competence to bring the war to an honorable end. As it turned out, Nixon and Kissinger were themselves shocked by the domestic reaction to their move, and the North Vietnamese leadership, apparently sensing this, only stiffened its intransigence at the negotiating table while intensifying its military efforts throughout Indochina.

The student protest movement, somewhat dormant since the election of Nixon, had been revived overnight by the news of the invasion of Cambodia. The combustible campus animosity toward the administration for its sluggish exit from Vietnam had been ignited into a firestorm of anger when four demonstrating students at Kent State University were killed by a trigger-happy Ohio National Guard unit. Efforts were intensified in Congress to limit the executive's war powers.

The Cambodian operation, conceived of as a means of widening U.S. options and limiting those of the North Vietnamese, had the opposite effect. Washington, not Hanoi, once again made the next concessions in the diplomatic arena—this time coming almost all the way toward the maximum demands of Hanoi.

Nixon now gave the go-ahead to propose a "cease-fire" even though the U.S. military and the U.S. embassy in Saigon believed this would put the Thieu regime in great physical jeopardy and in an untenable political position. "Cease-fire-in-place" was a euphemism for what was, in effect, an agreement to allow Hanoi to keep its forces in South Vietnam and to legitimize their hold on the territory they had already conquered. Here, finally, was the abandonment of the U.S. insistence on a mutual withdrawal of U.S. and North Vietnamese forces from the South. The U.S. forces alone would leave, being the only "foreign" forces there—a complete capitulation to Hanoi's insistence that the conflict in the South was a continuation of the civil war to liberate Vietnam from imperialism.

The Kalb brothers explain Nixon's turnaround on the basis of his new-found respect for the capabilities of the South Vietnamese military forces to fend for themselves against the communists, as had been demonstrated by their success in the invasion of Cambodia. An equally plausible explanation is that the White House finally decided to have done with the bloody mess.

Even such a fundamental concession was insufficient for the North Vietnamese, who, more contemptuous than ever of their opponents, would settle for nothing less than an American renunciation of the legitimacy of the Thieu regime. This last demand, from the administration's point of view, was surely irrational, for the cease-fire-in-place and accompanying interim political arrangements proposed to the North Vietnamese were clearly only face-saving mechanisms to allow the United States to get out before the final deposition of Thieu and the participation of the communists in the government in Saigon. Kissinger's military–diplomatic strategy from here on out was designed to convince Hanoi that (a) no matter how sick the United States was of the war, there was no possibility of persuading President Nixon to cooperate in the final humiliation of Thieu that Hanoi demanded, and (b) the United States was fully committed to a withdrawal of its own forces from Vietnam, and the cease-fire-in-place and interim political arrangements were not any kind of trick to put the North Vietnamese off balance.

The Mining of Haiphong Harbor: Attempts to Work the Moscow Connection

From the summer of 1970 through the spring of 1971, terrible pessimism pervaded Washington over the capacity of Nixon and Kissinger to gain that "peace with honor" that would allow the administration to finally get out of Vietnam. With the failure of either the Cambodia invasion or the post-Cambodia negotiating concessions to move Hanoi, Nixon and Kissinger appeared to have used up most of their available carrots and sticks.

The U.S. air support for the South Vietnamese army's 1971 incursion into Laos to cut the Ho Chi Minh trail network was a comparatively insignificant increment of coercion (Nixon was prevented by the Cooper-Church amendment from using U.S. ground forces, as he had in Cambodia). Moreover, the South Vietnamese troops were beaten back without accomplishing their mission.

Kissinger once again reached deep into his bag for two further initiatives in his secret negotiations with Le Duc Tho during the spring and summer of 1971: a promise that President Thieu would resign prior to internationally supervised elections under comprehensive peace arrangements, and assurances to Hanoi that all U.S. troops would be out of Vietnam within six months following the signing of the peace agreement. Le Duc Tho countered with his own nine points as the basis for continuing to negotiate in detail.[10] But by the fall of 1971, after six intense negotiating sessions in Paris, Kissinger and Le Duc Tho were still deadlocked over details—in essence, the inability of Kissinger and Nixon to agree to an unconditional surrender of South Vietnam. Le Duc Tho attempted to delegate the responsibility for further talks to his deputy. Kissinger's insistence that Le Duc Tho himself continue were ignored, so the negotiations were suspended.

Meanwhile, events along the great power nexus had been maturing. It was during the summer and fall of 1971 that Kissinger had arranged for Nixon's 1972 summit visits to Moscow and Peking; and it might now be possible to induce the communist giants, both of whom were competing for U.S. favor, to lean hard on their Vietnamese comrades to compromise with the United States. But Hanoi, perhaps sensing what was coming, began to lay the groundwork for a massive new invasion of the South. U.S. and South Vietnamese military commanders braced for an enemy offensive in February to coincide with the President's trip to China. Instead, Hanoi launched a major spring offensive across the demilitarized zone at the 17th parallel on March 31, a month after the Peking summit and seven weeks before the Moscow summit.

Nixon and Kissinger now moved to turn the screws on the Russians, to compel them to face the consequences for U.S.–Soviet relations of their continued support of the North Vietnamese war effort. State and Defense Department spokesmen began complaining publicly about the heavy role of Soviet military supplies in the new North Vientamese offensive.

Meanwhile, North Vietnam was brought under heavy and sustained air bombardment for the first time since the Johnson administration. The port of Haiphong and storage depots around Hanoi were raided by B-52s. Four Soviet merchant ships in

Haiphong Harbor were damaged by the bombings. U.S. officials hinted of still more destructive escalations to come, including even the mining of North Vietnamese ports which, by putting Soviet supply convoys in jeopardy, would force the issue with the Kremlin.

While the risks of a direct U.S.–Soviet confrontation over Vietnam rose to dangerous levels during April 1972, Kissinger traveled secretly to Moscow to firm up preparations for the May summit between Brezhnev and Nixon. As recounted in the preceding chapter, the evident progress in SALT and commercial talks gave both sides reason to hope for a major breakthrough in U.S.–Soviet relations to be unveiled at the summit as long as Vietnam did not ruin it. Each side sensed that the other was most anxious for the summit to take place. But as Kissinger was to find out in Moscow, since both were aware of the other's real priorities, neither could use the threat of postponing or canceling the summit as leverage on the other's role in Vietnam. Kissinger returned to Washington with plans for the May Nixon–Brezhnev meeting intact but with no meaningful Kremlin assurances to bring pressure on the Vietnamese to sign a compromise peace.

Two days after Kissinger returned from Moscow, Nixon went on nationwide televison and radio to vent his frustration at the lack of progress in the peace negotiations and to explain the reasons for the resumption of the systematic bombing of North Vietnam. The Easter weekend military offensive of the North, argued Nixon, had stripped away "whatever pretext there was of a civil war in South Vietnam." Once again escalating his rhetoric on the enormity of the international crime being committed by Hanoi, the President made it more difficult to admit, finally, that the United States had no business continuing to participate in the war: "What we are witnessing here, what is being brutally inflicted upon the people of South Vietnam, is a clear case of naked and unprovoked agression across an international border."[11] Curiously, this definition of the situation was revived after the United States had repeatedly offered to establish a cease-fire-in-place, to withdraw all its forces, and to establish interim political arrangements in the South based on the military status quo. Washington's willingness to legitimize the fruits of the war had thus already been established, even though at least ten regular North Vietnamese combat divisions were already in South Vietnam. Now Hanoi's movement of three additional combat divisions across the 17th parallel was pointed to as contradicting Hanoi's claim that the conflict was a civil war!

The reescalation of the U.S. stake in Vietnam was backed up by Nixon's promise to continue U.S. air and naval attacks on North Vietnam "until the North Vietnamese stop their offensive in South Vietnam."[12] Other officials hinted that more and more targets in the North would come under attack. Yet at the same time Nixon pledged to continue withdrawing American troops. He claimed to be able to do this because, according to reports he had received from the American commander in Vietnam, General Creighton Abrams, the South Vietnamese forces had demonstrated their ability to defend themselves on the ground against future enemy attacks. "I have decided," said the President, "that Vietnamization has proved itself sufficiently that we can continue our program of withdrawing American forces without detriment to our overall goal of insuring South Vietnam's survival as an independent country."[13]

However, the military reports from the field during the next few days did not support the President's optimistic assessment of the fighting capabilities of the South Vietnamese army. Abandoning Quangtri City, south of the 17th parallel, the South Vietnamese forces virtually turned and ran southward to avoid the advancing North Vietnamese. Hue would be next, and the resulting demoralization of Saigon would bring on a humiliating collapse of the South's effort before the 1972 presidential elections. Something had to be done to break the downhill slide.

Kissinger, again meeting with Le Duc Tho in Paris, offered to accelerate the U.S. withdrawal (all U.S. troops would be removed before the November elections) if Hanoi would agree to a ceasefire and a return of U.S. prisoners of war. In effect, he was saying: Just give us a decent interval to get out under the cloak of an apparent compromise, and you can have the whole country.

But riding high now, the North Vietnamese were evidently more confident than ever that they could have it entirely their way: The Americans would have to cooperate in immediately deposing the Thieu regime or else there would be no deal.

Nixon and Kissinger, still hoping to avoid wholesale capitulation to the communist demands, now attempted to use their incompletely exploited indirect leverage on Hanoi through the Moscow connection. The Navy was authorized to implement one of the favorite options of the Joint Chiefs of Staff: mining Haiphong harbor and other ports in order to drastically increase the risks and costs to the Soviets of supplying North Vietnam. Presumably, this would compel the Kremlin to lean hard on Hanoi to bring the war to an end through diplomacy instead of attempting to win a total military victory. The order to execute the operation was issued on May 8, 1972, only two weeks before Nixon was scheduled to meet with Brezhnev in Moscow. In so forcing the issue of Vietnam with the Russians, Nixon and Kissinger clearly were risking Kremlin postponement, if not cancelation, of the summit. It was a gamble, but Nixon claimed that his back was against the wall and he was left with no alternatives.

In his May 8, 1972, address explaining this decision, Nixon painted his options starkly: "immediate withdrawal of all American forces, continued attempts at negotiation, or decisive military action to end the war." The first course, he contended, "would mean turning 17 million South Vietnamese over to communist tyranny and terror. It would mean leaving hundreds of American prisoners in Communist hands with no bargaining leverage to get them released." And it would "encourage . . . smaller nations armed by their major allies . . . to attack neighboring nations at will in the Mideast, in Europe, and other areas."

The alternative of negotiating an honorable settlement was his preferred course, said Nixon. But after four years during which "we have made every reasonable offer and tried every possible path for ending this war at the conference table, . . . the North Vietnamese arrogantly refuse to negotiate anything but an . . .

ultimatum that the United States impose a Communist regime on 17 million people in South Viet-Nam.''

It was plain, Nixon concluded, ''that what appears to be a choice among three courses of action for the United States is really no choice at all. . . . There is only one way to stop the killing. That is to keep the weapons of war out of the hands of the international outlaws of North Vietnam''—in other words, a return to the first alternative, decisive military action:

> All entrances to North Vietnamese ports will be mined to prevent access to these ports and North Vietnamese naval operations from these ports.
>
> United States forces have been directed to take appropriate measures within the internal and claimed territorial waters of North Vietnam to interdict the delivery of any supplies.
>
> Rail and all other communications will be cut off to the maximum extent possible.
>
> Air and naval strikes against military targets in North Vietnam will continue.[14]

These acts of force would stop, promised the President, once U.S. prisoners of war were released by Hanoi and once an internationally supervised cease-fire had begun. At such time the United States would proceed to completely withdraw all its forces from Vietnam within four months.

Pointedly, Nixon began his address with special reference to the Soviet role. The present massive invasion of South Vietnam, he maintained, ''was made possible by tanks, artillery, and other advanced offensive weapons supplied to Hanoi by the Soviet Union and other Communist nations.'' And he closed with remarks directed at the Soviet leadership:

> We expect you to keep your allies, and you cannot expect us to do other than help our allies. But let us . . . help our allies only for the purpose of their defense, not for the purpose of launching invasions against their neighbors. . . .
>
> Our two nations have made significant progress in recent months. We are near major agreements on nuclear arms limitation, on trade, on a host of other issues. Let us not slide back toward the dark shadows of a previous age. . . .

> We, the United States and the Soviet Union, are on the threshold
> of a new relationship. . . . .We are prepared to build this rela-
> tionship. The responsibility is yours if we fail to do so.[15]

In this pointed rhetoric as well as in the military action, the May
1972 escalation was the biggest gamble Nixon took in Vietnam,
for it could have severely alienated the Russians on the eve of
the Moscow summit and thereby in one blow shattered the
larger diplomatic mosaic the administration was attempting to
construct.

The talk around Washington at the time, possibly inspired by
Kissinger himself, was that "Henry" opposed the President on
this one, and it was the vigorous intervention of Secretary of the
Treasury John Connally that stiffened the President's determination to up the ante despite the risks.[16]

It is not at all implausible that Kissinger, in order to keep his
diplomatic channels open, felt that it was tactically necessary to
separate himself somewhat from the administration's new bellig-
erent posture. Kissinger would be the one who would have to
reconstitute the summit plans if they were to fall apart temporarily, and it was Kissinger who still would have to meet face to face
with his North Vietnamese counterparts when the negotiations
resumed.

The basic escalatory ploy, however, was fully consistent with
the Kissinger mode of coercive diplomacy. In any event the gamble worked, at least insofar as the Kremlin chose not to scuttle
the larger détente relationship, and—to the surprise of most of
the Washington policy community—the Russians indicated that
the Nixon–Brezhnev summit was still on. But whether the gamble worked in its main objective of pressuring the Soviets to lean
hard on the North Vietnamese to finally negotiate a compromise
peace remains a question to be illuminated by further historical
research.

Defenders of the Haiphong mining operation claim not only
that it broke the back of North Vietnam's spring offensive but
that in driving up the risks to the Soviets themselves of a
prolongation of the war in Southeast Asia it was the key to a sig-

nificant Kremlin decision to reduce arms deliveries to North Vietnam and to President Nikolai Podgorny's visit to Hanoi of June 15, presumably to tell the North Vietnamese that they must now negotiate seriously to end the war instead of banking on a total capitulation by their opponents.[17]

If the Soviets did indeed intercede with Hanoi in the spring and summer of 1972 on behalf of the United States, they probably did so in order to continue the momentum of détente expressed at the Nixon–Brezhnev summit. There is no evidence, or logic, in the argument that they did so *because* of the Haiphong mining. Moreover, at the summit Kissinger and Nixon, it has been reported, inched even closer to Hanoi's maximum demands, reaffirming their acceptance of a North Vietnamese military presence in South Vietnam, endorsing a tripartite electoral commission that would include neutralists and the Viet Cong, and conveying their willingness to call off the bombing of the North prior to a release of American prisoners.[18]

During the summer and fall, Kissinger exhibited great optimism that the long-sought agreement with Hanoi to end the war was imminent. In retrospective interviews he attributed the intensification of constructive negotiations with Le Duc Tho to the success of his leverage diplomacy in putting pressure on both Moscow and Peking (each afraid the other would be favored by the United States) to persuade Hanoi to allow the Americans to leave Vietnam "with honor."[19]

The sequence of events supports a contrary explanation, namely, that Nixon and Kissinger, fearful of being outflanked in the coming U.S. presidential elections by a Democratic peace candidate, conveyed to the communist powers—more convincingly than ever before—their willingness to give in to Hanoi's demands on virtually all points. This interpretation is supported particularly by the evident reluctance of the White House to let the Thieu regime in Saigon know how completely the United States was now prepared to abandon South Vietnam. During the months following the Moscow summit, the problem of how to persuade Thieu to accept the inevitable became Washington's central preoccupation. White House military aide General Haig was dispatched to Saigon to persuade Thieu while Kissinger and Le Duc Tho labored through August, September, and October to dot the *i*'s and cross the *t*'s of what was now a basic Washington–Hanoi accord on most of the essential provisions of the peace agreement.

The Final Bravado

The hopes of Nixon and Kissinger to successfully conclude the peace negotiations on the eve of the November 1972 elections were dashed by Thieu's refusal to accept the terms agreed upon by Kissinger and Le Duc Tho. The South Vietnamese had numerous objections to the draft agreement, but their deepest grievances were over the establishment of a South Vietnamese coalition regime including the communists, and over the failure to provide for a withdrawal of North Vietnamese troops from South Vietnam. Kissinger urged the President to authorize a separate peace between the United States and North Vietnam; but Nixon needed Saigon's acquiescence to preserve the fiction of an "honorable peace." Accordingly, he had Kissinger delay the final signing. Hanoi thereupon unilaterally disclosed the terms of the draft agreement, probably in an effort to force the issue between Washington and Saigon. Kissinger maintained a public air of optimism by insisting that "peace is at hand," but he surely feared a last-minute disintegration of all of his painstaking labors.

When Kissinger and Le Duc Tho met again a few weeks after the November 1972 election, in which Nixon had defeated George McGovern by an overwhelming margin, the North Vietnamese negotiator seemed to have toughened his stand. Not only did he reject all the points Kissinger presented on behalf of President Thieu, but according to Kissinger's subsequent press briefings he made additional demands to alter the texts he and Kissinger had agreed to in October. In retrospect the new intransigence on the part of the North Vietnamese is understandable, for they could easily have interpreted Nixon's procrastination prior to the elections as a cover for the massive military reinforcements the United States flew into South Vietnam immediately after the election. Although the White House's purpose in this new military infusion may have been to buy off Thieu rather than to alter the military balance of power in South Vietnam before the cease-fire took effect, the North Vietnamese could well have suspected a ruse and decided to stall while engaging in their own compensatory reinforcements.

Nixon and Kissinger were more frustrated than ever. Had they slipped back on to a reverse track just as the opening at the end of the tunnel of war was immediately in front of them? Determined to break out at last, they tried one more dramatic set of moves. They now informed Hanoi that Nixon was ready to agree to a separate peace with North Vietnam if Thieu failed to agree to the October terms. They also informed Thieu of this decision and threatened to cut off all assistance to South Vietnam if Thieu persisted in being an obstructionist. Simultaneously, they delivered a 72-hour ultimatum to Hanoi that unless serious negotiations were resumed immediately they would bomb North Vietnam again with even less restraint than before. With the expiration of the ultimatum on December 18, U.S. bombers commenced a 12-day round-the-clock devastation attack on North Vietnam, including massive attacks on "military" targets in heavily populated areas of Hanoi and Haiphong.[20]

The 1972 Christmas bombing operation was nothing less than an effort to terrorize the North Vietnamese back to the negotiating table in a more contrite posture. Not incidentally, it would also impress President Thieu. After suffering a rain of bombs for nearly two weeks, the North Vietnamese said they had had enough; they were ready to resume serious negotiations. On December 30 Nixon ordered a halt to the attacks north of the 20th parallel and dispatched Kissinger to Paris for the diplomatic anticlimax.

On January 23, 1973, the Agreement on Ending the War and Restoring the Peace in Vietnam was initialed in Paris by Kissinger and Le Duc Tho. (On January 27 it was formally signed by Secretary of State William Rogers and the North Vietnamese foreign minister, Nguyen Duy Trinh, with the foreign minister of the Thieu regime and the foreign minister of the communist "Provisional Revolutionary Government" in South Vietnam separately countersigning special copies so that their two names would not appear together on any one document.) "The people of South Vietnam have been guaranteed the right to determine their own future without outside interference," announced President Nixon. "Throughout these negotiations we have been in closest consultation with President Thieu and other representatives of the Republic of South Vietnam. This settlement meets the goals and has the full support of President Thieu and the Government of the Republic of Vietnam, as well as that of our other allies who are affected."[21] Of course, neither the history of the negotiations nor the text of the 1973 agreement and attached protocols nor the subsequent fate of South Vietnam supported these claims by Nixon.

The Paris agreement and protocols were transparently a conditional surrender of the noncommunists to the communists in Vietnam. Coequal status was henceforth to be given in South Vietnam to the "two parties"—the Government of the Democratic Republic of Vietnam (the Thieu regime) and the Provisional Revolutionary Government of South Vietnam (the communists). The cease-fire would accordingly legitimize all communist military gains to date, and their continuing military–administrative control of these areas, pending the establishment of a new government of South Vietnam. The new government was to be established through "free and democratic general elections," but the two parties would each have a veto in all transitional processes and institutions leading toward the establishment of the new government. Meanwhile, the armed forces of the United States were to be totally withdrawn, regardless of whether the political–governmental provisions of the agreement were working. There was no requirement, however, for the North Vietnamese to remove their forces. Some weak and ambiguous controls were provided on the military reinforcement by North Vietnam and the United States of their respective South Vietnamese allies, but the interpretation and enforcement of these controls would also be subject to the veto of both parties. Kissinger did succeed in getting the North Vietnamese to concede to most of the U.S. demands for the prompt return of all captured military personnel and foreign civilians; this was accomplished by putting the provision on the return of captured Vietnamese civilians in a separate article stipulating that the question "will be resolved by the two South Vietnamese parties."[22]

To the surprise of no one who knew the situation in Indochina, the paper peace began to crumble before its ink was dry. Both sides violated the strictures against new military buildups; each blamed the other for the renewed outbreak of fighting and, of course, for the failure to set up institutions to govern the transition to free elections. The military balance of power in South Vietnam, Laos, and Cambodia continued to determine the future of these countries, given the prevailing political anarchy in each. Kissinger, realpolitician as he was, could not have expected anything else. What did surprise him, perhaps, was the Soviets' continuation of their heavy military supply effort to the Vietnamese communists. Kissinger and President Ford made their obligatory pleas to a reluctant Congress to match the Soviet effort; but even as the final panic spread in South Vietnam in the spring of 1975 there were few Americans in political life who would define the situation in Vietnam as sufficiently vital to U.S. interests to justify still another futile pretense of honor.

4

☆☆☆THE MIDDLE EAST AND THE REASSERTION OF AMERICAN COMPETENCE ABROAD

> I am wandering around here like a rug merchant in order to bargain over 100 to 200 meters! Like a peddler in the market! I'm trying to save you, and you think you are doing me a favor when you are kind enough to give me a few more meters.
> Henry A. Kissinger to the Israelis in 1974 *

For Nixon and Kissinger the liquidation of the Vietnam war was the precondition for the restoration of American international power. They regarded détente with the Soviet Union and rapprochement with China as conducive to the revival of domestic and foreign belief in America's dedication to peace and world order, and in its "vision" (a favorite Kissinger word). It was in the Middle East, however, that Nixon and Kissinger could prove the capacity and will to *use* American power effectively during crises in the service of peace and order and, by so doing, re-create international respect for the United States as a constructive and competent superpower.

Their principal Middle Eastern challenges—countering the Soviet buildup of Egyptian military power, controlling the Jordanian crisis of 1970, and stage-managing the termination of the

---

* Quoted by Matti Golan, *The Secret Conversations of Henry Kissinger: Step-by-Step Diplomacy in the Middle East* (New York: Quadrangle/New York Times Books, 1976), p. 195.

1973 Arab–Israeli war—provided both men with the opportunity to manipulate the most awesome components of American power. Particularly in the 1973–1974 crisis period, as Nixon became more preoccupied with Watergate, it was Kissinger who had to direct the major military as well as political moves; and by all accounts he loved it.

Kissinger had reason to rate his Mideast diplomacy as eminently successful: After the Israeli victories of 1967 the Russians had increased their influence with the Arabs, but the United States emerged from the crises of 1970–1974 as the most influential external power. And in a situation that was widely regarded as the most likely tinderbox for igniting World War III, the Nixon and Ford administrations were instrumental in containing and terminating local conflagrations that could have exploded into global holocaust.

Credit must be given to the role played by the United States during the Kissinger years in defining the permissible bounds of action for all actors and providing external sanctions to the local antagonists to resolve their differences through diplomacy rather than war. When it came to a more permanent impact on the situation, however, in the sense of ameliorating the chronic sources of dangerous conflict in the Middle East or leaving intact a system of conflict controls that would reduce the prospects of major war, Kissinger had less basis for pride that he had made a historic contribution to international order.

The Failure of Peace Diplomacy in 1969 and 1970

The Nixon administration inherited the basic dilemma of U.S. Middle Eastern policy: By guaranteeing Israel's security against Arab aggression, the United States had driven many countries into the arms of the Soviet Union and made it more difficult for pro-U.S. regimes in the area to sustain themselves in the face of radical domestic movements. But if the United States were to reduce its support for Israel, the Arabs, with Soviet backing, might soon come to believe they could overpower the small Jewish state. The crushing of Israel would be intolerable to the United States, and its prevention would require U.S. counter-moves that would increase the likelihood of a U.S.–Soviet military clash.

Upon assuming the Presidency, Nixon attempted to transcend this dilemma by making the United States the active catalyst of the peace process in the Middle East. New initiatives were taken on two levels simultaneously: (a) intense U.S.–Soviet consultations designed to lock the Russians into a joint approach toward an Arab-Israeli settlement and (b) a new "evenhanded" posture toward the demands of the Israelis and the Arabs. Both were reflected in what came to be known as the Rogers plan—the U.S. draft outline of an Arab–Israeli settlement presented by Secretary of State William R. Rogers to the Soviets for Kremlin endorsement as agreed-upon terms of reference for more specific peace negotiations between Israel and Egypt.

In his memoirs Nixon recalls the thinking behind the new initiatives. "If the Soviets were committed to Arab victories and we were committed to Israeli victories, it did not require much imagination to see how both might be drawn in even against our wills—and almost certainly against our national interests." Whether or not the Kremlin could be enticed into a constructive diplomatic process, it was clearly in America's interest "to halt the Soviet domination of the Arab Mideast. To do so would require broadening American relations with the Arab countries. Within the first few weeks of my administration I began taking the first steps in this direction."[1]

The new approach rested on two assumptions that turned out to be untenable—or at least premature: (a) that the Kremlin too was increasingly apprehensive that the superpowers' competitive support of their respective Middle Eastern clients could lead to a direct U.S.–Soviet military clash, and therefore might be willing to trade the presence it was gaining from a polarization of the area in return for coequal status with the United States as joint peacemaker, and (b) that a posture of U.S. impartiality toward the Arabs and Israel would give the Nixon administration greater leverage over *both* sides than continuation of the past pro-Israel policies. The first assumption crumbled as evidence mounted in 1969 and 1970 of a continuing enlargement of the Soviet military presence in Egypt coupled with the buildup of the Russian navy in the Mediterranean, and it was discarded when it became clear at the end of the year that the Kremlin was exerting little if any pressure on Nasser to negotiate a compromise peace. The second assumption, even though apparently contradicted by Israel's categorical rejection of the Rogers plan as an "imposed" peace, was never adequately tested during this period. Soviet–Egyptian collusion in the military sphere, and then the Jordanian crisis, pushed the larger peace diplomacy aside and drove the United States back into the role of overt guarantor of Israeli security. In 1969 Russian military assistance was proceeding beyond simply replacing Egyptian losses in the Six Day War. The buildup now included modern surface-to-air missiles (SAM) that might negate Israel's air superiority and thus shift the balance of power toward the Arabs, whose overwhelming military manpower advantage could eventually make the difference in a ground war. Indeed, the Egyptians were becoming more daring in the spring of 1969 in their military raids across the Suez Canal into Israeli-occupied territory along the east bank, portending Nasser's flirtation with the idea of launching a major cross-canal invasion under the cover of Soviet antiaircraft sites on the west bank. Israel, predictably, asked for additional U.S. fighter aircraft to compensate for the improvements in Egypt's air defense capabilities. To those who bought the premises of the Nixon–Rogers diplomatic initiatives, however, these military trends only underlined the urgency of efforts to get the Egyptians committed to negotiations with Israel and the Israelis committed to relinquishing most of the territory they had conquered in 1967.

The starting point for the proposed negotiations was United Nations Resolution 242, an ambiguous set of principles passed by the Security Council on November 22, 1967, that both Israel and Egypt said they accepted. Resolution 242 called for a settlement based on "withdrawal of Israeli armed forces from territories occupied in the recent June 1967 conflict" and "termination of all claims or states of belligerency and respect for and acknowledgement of the sovereignty, territorial integrity, and political independence of every state in the area and their right to live in peace within secure and recognized boundries free from threats or acts of force."[2]

Implementation of Resolution 242 had stalled during the last fourteen months of the Johnson administration, primarily over differing interpretations of the sequencing of the Israeli withdrawals and the full recognition of Israel's legitimacy by the Arabs. The Arabs, backed by the Soviets, had been insisting on withdrawal first, then peace. The Israelis, supported at least implicitly by the United States, regarded Arab acceptance of Israel as the necessary precondition for relinquishment of territories conquered during the last round of the war. The two sides also disagreed over how much of the conquered territory Israel was obligated to give back.

President Nixon delegated Secretary of State Rogers to try to resolve the impasse through a series of diplomatic initiatives aimed at the Soviet Union, the Arabs, and Israel that would compress and dissipate the question of timing in a package of detailed provisions on the rights and duties of the local parties that would form the context for Israeli withdrawals. "To call for Israeli withdrawal as envisaged in the U.N. resolution without achieving agreement on peace would be partisan toward the Arabs," explained Secretary Rogers. "To call on the Arabs to accept peace without Israeli withdrawal would be partisan toward Israel. Therefore, our policy is to encourage the Arabs to accept a permanent peace based on a binding agreement and to urge the Israelis to withdraw from occupied territory when their territorial integrity is assured as envisaged by the Security Council resolution."[3]

The most fully worked out version of the Rogers Plan, as presented to the Soviets on October 28, 1969, provided for indirect negotiations between Israel and Egypt and outlined the key provisions of the agreement that should ensue: (a) a timetable, to be agreed upon during the negotiations, for withdrawal of Israeli forces from Egyptian territory occupied during the 1967 war; (b) a formal end to the state of war; (c) specification of the precise locations of the agreed-upon "secure borders," and the establishment of demilitarized zones; (d) freedom of navigation through the Strait of Tiran and an affirmation of its status as an international waterway; (e) nondiscriminatory navigation for the ships of all nations, including Israel, through the Suez Canal; (f) a final settlement of the Gaza strip issue; (g) participation in a process for resolving the Palestinian refugee problem; (h) mutual recognition of each other's sovereignty, political independence, and right to live in peace within secure boundries free from threats of force; and (i) submission of the final document to the UN Security Council for ratification, and to the United States, the Soviet Union, Great Britain, and France, which would promise to help both sides adhere to the agreement.[4] In December the United States presented to the Big Four a parallel plan outlining a Jordanian–Israeli agreement, including provisions for Jordan's sharing in the administration of Jerusalem.

Despite the elaborate surrounding diplomacy—a preliminary series of meetings on earlier drafts with the Russians, U.S. soundings with Israel, and Soviet soundings with Egypt—the Rogers initiatives got nowhere. Israel flatly rejected the "attempt to impose a forced solution on her . . . [and] appease them [the Arabs] at the expense of Israel."[5] The Soviets, unable to deliver the Egyptians, also rejected the Rogers plan.

In retrospect, Nixon claims to have known that the provisions for returning the occupied territories to the Arabs meant that "the Rogers Plan had absolutely no chance of being accepted by Israel." He also presents himself as being (privately) closer to the realistic persuasion of Kissinger, who not only predicted the Israeli rejection but also argued that the plan would encourage Arab extremists and naively play into the hands of the Soviets. "I knew that the Rogers Plan could never be implemented," writes Nixon,

> but I believed that it was important to let the Arab world know that the United States did not automatically dismiss its case regarding

the occupied territories or rule out a compromise settlement of the conflicting claims. With the Rogers Plan on the record, I thought it would be easier for the Arab leaders to propose reopening relations with the United States without coming under attack from the hawks and pro-Soviet elements in their own countries.[6]

Kissinger's influence on U.S. policy during the period of the Rogers plan appears to have been shadowy but substantial. On the basis of Nixon's published recollections and detailed journalistic accounts, the popular notion that Kissinger took little interest in Middle Eastern affairs until the 1973 Yom Kippur War is unwarranted.

The Nixon administration took office amid rumors that a new round of hostilities was imminent. A National Security Study Memorandum—NSSM-2—on the Middle Eastern situation was ordered by Kissinger early in January 1969 and delivered to him the day after inauguration. Nixon's decision to have the United States take an active role in the peace diplomacy was based on one of the main policy options in this document, the option reportedly favored by Kissinger. Moreover, while Secretary of State Rogers and Assistant Secretary Joseph Sisco began the process of sounding out all parties to a potential settlement, Kissinger, according to journalist Tad Szulc, was working with Soviet Ambassador Dobrynin to institute a secret top-level dialog on the Middle East between the White House and the Kremlin, in keeping with the Nixon–Kissinger philosophy that a settlement required the exercise of substantial leverage by both the Soviet Union and the United States over their respective clients. Tangible leverage presumably existed on both sides in the form of controls over the transfer and witholding of military aid by Russia to Egypt and by the United States to Israel.[7]

From the point of view of Secretary of State Rogers and others who favored the policy of evenhandedness, the rejection by Israel and the Soviet Union of the Rogers plan in late 1969 was due in part to the failure of President Nixon and his principal national security adviser to give it their firm backing. This was undoubtedly the case; but the more important question for the purposes of our analysis is why Nixon and Kissinger encouraged

Rogers to proceed as far as he did while they themselves were only lukewarm toward the initiative.

One explanation is that the White House harbored no illusions about the Kremlin's motivation to oppose any real movement toward genuine peace as something that would reduce Soviet influence in the Middle East; yet the Rogers plan was a vehicle for putting the Russians on the defensive and showing the Arabs that if there was to be any diplomatic leverage on Israel to return the conquered territories, it was from Washington, not Moscow, that it would have to come. Another explanation is that Nixon and Kissinger knew that Golda Meir's government would find the plan an unacceptable trade of Israeli physical security for Arab assurances, the latter being wholly unreliable so soon after the Arab humiliation of 1967; yet the initiative would give the policy of evenhandedness credibility with the Arabs—hence the elaborate efforts to keep the details of the U.S. proposals from the Israelis and the U.S. Jewish community. (This explanation is consistent with the White House's having let Rogers finally reveal the contents of his latest draft proposals in a major address in December 1969, with Nixon and Kissinger knowing full well that the outraged reaction from Israel and its U.S. supporters would consign the Rogers plan to the State Department's file of misfired initiatives.) Another, even more cynical, explanation is that Nixon and Kissinger, knowing that the Arabists in the State Department had built up a full head of steam in preparation for implementing the policy of evenhandedness, saw the Rogers approach as a way of distracting the State Department from the real game of balance-of-power politics that the President wanted to play personally from the Oval Office.

White House actions surrounding the Rogers plan are consistent with all of these explanations; and all of them, indeed, may accurately reflect the thinking of Nixon and Kissinger at the time. They are also consistent with Kissinger's retrospective remark to the Kalbs that "I always thought there had to be a period of stalemate in which the various parties recognize the limits of what they could achieve."[8] Kissinger's comment provides a context for understanding the most concrete element in U.S. policy toward the Arab–Israeli conflict during this period, namely, the Nixon administration's responses to the requests by the Meir government for new fighter aircraft to counter the Soviet build-up of Egyptian military capabilities.

The Israelis were asking for 80 A-4 Skyhawks and 25 F-4 Phantoms.[9] Some token deliveries, made in secret in the fall of 1969, were far short of previous Israeli requests and expectations; and the administration acted slowly in deciding how to respond to the new requests. The Israelis, of course, were anxious to maintain decisive military superiority; but for the Americans to substantially acquiesce to the Israeli requests would only mean that the Kremlin would feel compelled to respond to Arab requests to further enlarge Soviet deliveries in the area. From the White House perspective, it was important to maintain a deterrent balance, but at the lowest level of outside provisioning possible. A not incidental side benefit from the U.S. policy of maintaining a restrictive hand on the spigot controlling the flow of arms to Israel was the reminder it provided to the Israelis that it was necessary for them to act in consonance with Washington's basic Mideast policies if they wished to maintain an adequate military posture toward the Arabs.

Neither the Soviets nor the Arabs, however, chose to credit the restrained U.S. arms transfer policy in late 1969 as a genuine indication that the United States was ready to use its influence to compel Israel to give up the occupied territories. They focused primarily on the continuing role of the United States as Israel's military guarantor, and alleged that by helping to reduce Israel's military vulnerability the United States was reducing Israeli incentives to part with the conquered territory.

In January 1970, as the Israeli air force began to step up its raids on Egypt in retaliation for the persisting Egyptian forays across the canal, the process of polarization and competitive arming eclipsed the peace efforts. Raw balance-of-power calculations once again dominated the Middle Eastern scene and the deliberations in the White House. On January 31 Nixon received what Kissinger termed the "first Soviet threat" of his administration—a letter from Premier Kosygin stating that "we would like to tell you in all frankness that if Israel continues its adventurism, to bomb the territory of the UAR and other Arab states, the Soviet Union will be forced to see to it that the Arab states have the means at their disposal, with the help of which a due rebuff to the arrogant aggressor could be made."[10]

Nixon's reply to the threatening Kosygin letter was, by his own characterization, "carefully low-keyed." He urged the Kremlin to be more positive in its response to the Rogers plan and also proposed U.S.–Soviet discussions on limiting arms supplies to the Middle East.[11] Meanwhile, he continued to postpone responding to Israel's requests for new jet aircraft deliveries. But in the spring of 1970 the deterioration was advancing too rapidly both on the superpower level and on Israel's border to be arrested by benign pleas for cooperation. In April U.S. and Israeli intelligence sources were picking up signs not only that the Soviets were accelerating their deliveries of SAMs, supersonic jets, and tanks to Egypt but also that Russian military personnel were beginning to man some of the SAM sites and fly some of the planes. Nixon ordered a full investigation of the expanding Soviet role and quietly stepped up the flow of U.S. military supplies to Israel; but he still held back on approving delivery of the supersonic planes that the Israelis were now urgently demanding.[12]

As the situation along the Suez became more threatening to Israel, Nixon played on Israeli entreaties for a more forthcoming U.S. response to its military equipment requirements by asking the Israelis to exhibit more flexibility in their terms for a settlement. At the end of May, Prime Minister Meir reiterated Israel's acceptance of Resolution 242 and agreed that it should be the basis of indirect talks between Israel and the UAR. Washington next pressed for an Arab–Israeli cease-fire while talks between the Israelis and Egyptians were conducted under the auspices of UN Special Ambassador Gunnar Jarring. To overcome Israeli fears that a cease-fire would only be exploited by the Russians and Arabs to further strengthen Arab military capabilities, Nixon assured Meir that the United States would continue its arms deliveries at whatever level was needed to prevent a shift in the local balance of power; to that end, in early July he authorized the shipment of electronic-countermeasure (ECM) equipment for Israeli jets to help Israel overcome the Soviet SAMs in the canal zone.[13]

The Israelis were not at all pleased with these marginalist and temporizing responses to their requests for decisive U.S. diplomatic and military backing at a time, as they saw it, of increasing peril to their very existence. And they continued to express deep skepticism about Arab motives in any cease-fire. The Israelis feared that the Arabs would use the cease-fire not, as the Americans hoped, as a transition to a negotiated peace but, rather, as additional time for completing their military build-up while forestalling a major new round of U.S. military supplies to Israel.

The strongest statement of American intentions during this period came from Kissinger in a June 26 background briefing at San Clemente. "We are trying to get a settlement in such a way that the moderate regimes are strengthened, and not the radical regimes," he told a group of newspaper editors. "We are trying to *expel* the Soviet military presence, not so much the advisers, but the combat pilots and combat personnel, before they become so firmly established."[14]

Egypt was the first to accept the American cease-fire proposal—on July 22, 1970, more than a month after Rogers proposed it. Jordan accepted on July 26. Israel reluctantly acquiesced on August 6. August 7 marked the first day of the cease-fire, which was supposed to last three months and to include a military standstill in a zone thirty-two miles wide on each side of the Suez Canal.

When the Israelis almost immediately began to report Egyptian violations of the truce, in the form of a continuing movement of SAM batteries into the standstill zone, the State Department was unimpressed and characterized the Israeli evidence as "inconclusive." But U.S. reconnaissance flights soon confirmed that the Egyptians were indeed systematically introducing new missile launchers into the prohibited area. On August 22 the administration informed the Soviet Union and Egypt that it had "incontrovertible evidence" of the violations, and it followed this up on September 3 by presenting the Russians and the Egyptians with evidence that at least fourteen missile sites had been modified between August 15 and August 27.[15]

Nixon now decided to sell Israel at least eighteen of the F-4 supersonic aircraft it had requested. He also ordered rush deliveries to Israel of the latest ECM equipment and conventional Shrike air-to-ground missiles so that the Israeli air force could neutralize the SAMs.

At least as important as the resumption of a major flow of U.S. military supplies to Israel was the impact of the Russian–Egyptian violations of the canal zone truce on the Nixon administration's general policy. There was now a decided tilt toward the Israelis, and a new sympathy for the Meir government's reluctance to make territorial concessions in advance of public and tangible commitments from Egypt indicating plans to live in peace with the Jewish state. Nixon and Kissinger also were freshly determined to reduce Soviet influence over the Arabs and were on the lookout for opportunities to demonstrate American coercive power in the region. Such an opportunity came somewhat sooner than expected.

The Jordan Crisis

September 1970 was the month of maximum trauma for King Hussein, and the situation in Jordan presented Nixon and Kissinger with their first full-blown Middle Eastern crisis.

King Hussein was not only the most pro-Western of Arab leaders but also the most cooperative when it came to working for a compromise Arab–Israeli peace. As a consequence he was on the enemies list of the militant anti-Israelis in the region, particularly the Palestinian commando organizations that wanted to use Jordan's western border areas as a staging ground for raids into Israel. Moreover, many of the radical Palestinians living in Jordan were determined to destroy the Hussein regime and make Jordan the center of their drive to regain the Palestinian lands now controlled by Israel and to push the Jews into the sea.

On September 6, members of the Popular Front for the Liberation of Palestine (PFLP) hijacked a TWA plane and a Swissair plane and forced them to land on an airstrip in Jordan twenty-five miles from the capital, Amman. A third airliner was captured and flown to Cairo, where its passengers were unloaded just before the plane was blown up. Still another plane, a BOAC jet, was hijacked the next day and also flown to the Jordanian airstrip, giving the PFLP a total of 475 hostages, many of them Americans, in Jordan. The hijackers threatened to blow up the three planes with their passengers aboard unless all Palestinian and pro-Palestinian prisoners in Israel, West Germany, Britain, and Switzerland were released. Beyond this ostensible purpose, the PFLP motive seemed to be to humiliate the Jordan monarchy, paving the way for a Palestinian takeover of the government in Amman. King Hussein was in a double bind: If he failed to move decisively, the Jordanian army might take matters into its own hands, thereby undercutting his authority. Yet he was reluctant to order the army to storm the airstrip, apparently not so much out of fear that the hostages would be killed as out of anxiety that Syria or Iraq might move forces into Jordan on behalf of the Palestinians.[16]

Hussein's dilemma, however, meshed with Nixon's determination to show resolve and to inject the United States more directly into the Middle East scene as a counter to the increasing Soviet participation. U.S. paratroopers of the 82d Airborne Division were placed on semialert status; a fleet of C-130 air transports was dispatched to Turkey under an escort of F-4 jet fighters for possible use in evacuating the Americans from Jordan; and units of the Mediterranean Sixth Fleet were ordered to sail toward the coasts of Israel and Lebanon.

On September 12, six days after the hijacking began, the PFLP transfered the hostages to some of their camps and blew up the three empty planes. In exchange for an Israeli agreement to release 450 Palestinian prisoners, the hijackers began releasing the hostages but continued temporarily to hold 55 Jewish passengers.[17]

Three days later what started out as an extortionary ploy exploded into a raging international crisis with the risk of a direct U.S.–Soviet clash. While holding the hostages in the desert, the PFLP stepped up terrorist attacks against the royal forces. On September 15 the King replaced his civilian officials with a military government, signaling his decision to move in force against the guerilla strongholds. Jordan was now in a state of civil war.

The immediate question in Washington was whether Syria and Iraq would intervene. The intelligence community tended to discount the likelihood of such intervention but Nixon spoke and acted as if he considered it imminent. On September 16, in an off-the-record briefing to a group of midwestern newspaper editors, he said that the United States might have to intervene if Syria or Iraq threatened Hussein. The *Chicago Sun Times* published some of the President's remarks and, surprisingly, was complimented by Nixon for breaking the ground rules. Clearly, Nixon wanted his implied warning to be picked up not only in Arab capitals but also in Moscow. Similar intense concern and hints of U.S. involvement were expressed by Kissinger and Assistant Secretary of State Sisco in background briefings that the press could attribute to "administration officials."[18] The verbal signaling was underscored by a set of military decisions: the aircraft carrier *John F. Kennedy* was ordered into the Mediterranean and the helicopter carrier *Guam*, loaded with 1,500 marines, dispatched from Norfolk, Virginia, in the direction of the Middle East. Nixon also authorized half a billion dollars in military aid for Israel and an acceleration of fighter aircraft deliveries.[19]

Nixon recollects his considerations at the time as follows:

> We would not allow Hussein to be overthrown by a Soviet-inspired insurrection. If it succeeded, the entire Middle East might erupt in war; the Israelis would almost certainly take pre-emptive measures against a Syrian-dominated radical government in Jordan; the Egyptians were tied to Syria by military alliances; and Soviet prestige was on the line with both Syria and the Egyptians. Since the United States could not stand idly by and watch Israel driven into the sea, the possibility of a direct U.S.–Soviet confrontation was uncomfort-

ably high. It was like a ghastly game of dominoes, with a nuclear war waiting at the end.[20]

On September 18 Kissinger was informed by both the Israeli ambassador, Yitzhak Rabin, and the Jordanian ambassador, Abdul Hamis Sharaf, that some Syrian tanks had crossed into Jordan and were headed toward the city of Irbid. Kissinger had Sisco check with the Russians, who offered their assurances that the Syrians had not invaded Jordan. And the State Department received a communication from Moscow telling of the Kremlin's efforts to prevent any outside intervention by Jordan's neighbors.

The next day the White House received firmer evidence that the Syrians had indeed invaded, and it was not a small probe. Some hundreds of tanks were now rolling toward Irbid. Kissinger is reported to have been furious at the Russians for attempting to deceive him and the President. The Kremlin must have been aware of what was happening and perhaps had even urged the Syrians on, for Syrian tank units were known to have Soviet military advisers. Having spent a good part of the day presiding over an emergency meeting of the Washington Special Action Group in the White House Situation Room, Kissinger reported on the fast-breaking crisis to the President and recommended an alert of American forces. Nixon agreed and ordered a selective alert of American troops in the United States and Western Europe. The alert included the 82d Airborne Division at Fort Bragg and U.S. airborne units in West Germany—the latter crossing the Autobahn conspicuously on their way to the airfields. "We wanted to get picked up" by Soviet intelligence, Kissinger later told the Kalb brothers. The Sixth Fleet was also augmented, and the ships with marine corps fighting units aboard steamed ominously toward the coasts of Israel and Lebanon. These military moves were coupled with U.S. warnings to the Russians that if the Syrians did not withdraw from Jordan the Israelis might intervene and the United States itself might not be able to stay out.[21]

On September 20 and 21, the Syrians continued to pour military forces into Jordan. Either the U.S. countermoves had not registered or Damascus, with Moscow's backing, had determined that the Americans were bluffing. But in truth Nixon and Kissinger were deadly serious. The crisis edged further toward the brink of major international war as King Hussein requested Israeli air support and the Israelis in turn asked for U.S. protection in the event that such Israeli intervention provoked an Egyptian/Russian counterintervention. Additional U.S. military forces in Germany were placed on alert, and transport planes were readied to airlift them to the Middle East. The augmented Sixth Fleet moved in closer. As an indicator of U.S.–Israeli coordination, a small U.S. intelligence aircraft flew back and forth between the advance naval units and Tel Aviv, with the Russians obviously watching.

Finally, the Israelis and Jordanians got the presidential decisions they were waiting for: if Israel were attacked by Egyptian and Soviet forces in response to its military help to King Hussein, the United States would itself intervene militarily to oppose them. On September 22, emboldened by confidence that Israel would indeed join the battle and would be backed by the United States, Hussein threw his own ground and air forces fully against the Syrians. The crisis suddenly broke. Syrian tanks began turning around and moving back toward Syria.[22]

Triumphant, Nixon flew to Rome a few days later and spent a night on the aircraft carrier *Saratoga* in the Mediterranean to symbolize his renewed pride in the potency of American military power as a diplomatic instrument. Kissinger—prudently—did not share the limelight.

From their management of the Jordan crisis, Nixon and Kissinger apparently drew some lessons for the conduct of their subsequent Middle Eastern policy—lessons that turned them away from the evenhandedness associated with the Rogers plan and back toward the more openly pro-Israel diplomacy of previous administrations. Indeed, until the 1973 Yom Kippur war and Arab oil embargo compelled them once again to reexamine the basic assumptions of this policy, Israel was treated as a virtual ally (along with Jordan, Iran, and Saudi Arabia) against a coalition of pro-Soviet states including Egypt, Syria, Iraq, and Libya. During this period, while the global pattern of international alignments was loosening under détente and rapid socioeconomic and political change was undermining any such simplistic division of the Middle East, the Nixon administration rather complacently trusted to regional polarization, backed up by Israeli and Iranian military superiority, to stabilize the area. Indications of divisions in the regional pro-Soviet coalition— most notably the decision of Anwar Sadat to expel some 10,000 Soviet military advisers from Egypt in July 1972—were seen not as evidence of the anachronism of the regional bipolar balance of power but, rather, as evidence of its success: Sadat was regarded as increasingly frustrated at the insufficient support he was getting from the Russians, who were presumably wary of backing him in further military adventures, given the new solidity of the U.S.–Israel political and military relationship.

The Yom Kippur War

"The news of the imminent attack on Israel took us completely by surprise," recalls Nixon.[23] This admission itself would not be surprising if it simply referred to the jarring effect the news had on Nixon personally. For the President was already up to his neck in the Watergate tapes by the morning of October 6, 1973, and was also trying to decide how to handle the legal charges of corruption being brought against Vice President Spiro Agnew. But the surprise went deeper, reflecting a massive intelligence failure in the U.S. government, which in turn was caused less by lack of hard information on the preparatory moves of Egypt and its allies than by the assumptions through which Kissinger and Nixon had processed all information coming out of the Middle East since 1970.

At the height of the crisis, Kissinger made a most revealing comment about the failure of both Israeli and U.S. intelligence (and therefore his own failure) to spot what was about to take place:

> Nobody made any mistakes about the facts. There are always two
> aspects to intelligence. One is a determination of the facts; the
> other is the interpretation of these facts. And there is the tendency
> of most intelligence services—and indeed most senior officials and
> indeed of some newspapermen—to fit the facts into existing pre-
> conceptions and to make them consistent with what is anticipated.
> And if you start from the assumption that a war is probably un-
> likely—if you know that there have been Egyptian maneuvers every
> September over the last 10 years—then there is probably a ten-
> dency to make observed facts fit your preconceived theories. . . .
>
> Over the years that I have been in this position, the possibility of
> a massive Arab attack was not considered among the most likely by
> any of the evaluators that I have talked to.[24]

The administration's bedrock assumption was that war was a
wholly unattractive alternative to the Egyptians as long as Israel
maintained effective superiority and there was a good prospect
that it would return the occupied territories as a result of international political pressure. Egypt and Syria might threaten war
from time to time, but this was only a ploy to intensify the international pressure on Israel to make concessions.

The premises may have been correct; but even so, they
begged the question of how Egypt might assess the pertinent
military balance at any time, which would include its judgments
about the willingness of other countries to come to the aid of
the belligerents in case of war. They also left as a variable the
degree of Egyptian optimism concerning Israel's willingness to
part with territory. In the final analysis the probability of a new
Mideast war was to a large extent determined by highly subjec-
tive Egyptian judgments that could shift in response to the dy-
namic political and military situation.

Another unstable variable was Soviet policy. Kissinger and
Nixon, however, assumed that the Soviets were firmly opposed
to a new round of war between the Arabs and the Israelis. The
Kremlin might still be attempting to gain influence among the
Arabs from a no-war-no-peace situation, but a hot war could
draw in the USSR and the United States on opposite sides, and
this might spell the end of détente. Brezhnev was thought to

have too much at stake in détente to put it at risk on behalf of his Middle Eastern clients. And being the military supplier of Egypt and Syria, he was in a position to pull the reins on any reckless action they might contemplate. The possibility that Soviet policy might be catalyzed by indigenous Middle Eastern factors, rather than the other way around, was presumably discounted in the White House, as was the possibility that the Soviet leaders might be so confident about the durability of the détente relationship in arms control and commerce that they could countenance a war between the Middle Eastern clients of the two superpowers.

Thus, it was the general orientation of those at the highest levels of the U.S. government that was responsible for misreading and underweighting of a series of specific developments that, in retrospect, look like inexorable moves toward the October 1973 war: [25]

- On November 14, 1972, Anwar Sadat promised the Higher Council of his Arab Socialist Union party that Egypt would attack Israel sometime within the coming twelve months.
- During the winter of 1972–1973, Egypt and the USSR seemed to be repairing their rift, which had led Sadat to expel all Soviet military advisers and experts the previous July and to place all Soviet bases and equipment in Egypt under exclusive Egyptian control. Egypt now invited back several hundred Soviet military advisers and allowed the Russians once again to use military facilities in Egypt. In return Brezhnev agreed to substantially increase the flow of Soviet military equipment to Egypt, this time apparently in some categories that he was reluctant to include earlier, such as the advanced SAM-6 mobile antiaircraft missile. The deliveries also included bridge-building equipment.
- In the spring Sadat began a series of intensive consultations with King Faisal of Saudi Arabia, who in recent months had been hinting strongly that he was ready to use his oil

assets as a political weapon against the friends of Israel, and with President Hafez Assad of Syria, the most prominent war hawk in the Arab camp.

• In June reports reached Washington of a massive acceleration of Russian arms deliveries to Syria, including late-model T-62 tanks, sophisticated antitank missiles, SAMs, and MIG-21 fighters.

• In the second week of September, King Hussein of Jordan flew to Cairo for a summit meeting with Sadat and Assad. Reports on the meeting indicated that war contingencies were discussed.

• During the last week of September, CIA reports to Kissinger spotlighted a number of unusual Egyptian, Syrian, and Soviet military movements. The annual Egyptian military maneuvers (which Kissinger later mentioned in his October 12 news conference) were being conducted with full divisions of Egyptian troops this time. Not only were the Egyptians stockpiling more ammunition and logistical support than ever before; they were also setting up a field communications network more complicated than mere maneuvers would require. The CIA analysts pointed to simultaneous suspicious deployments of Syrian tanks out of their normal defensive formations. U.S. surveillance also detected three Soviet freighters on their way to Egypt, possibly loaded with surface-to-surface missiles that could hit Israeli cities from Egyptian territory. Similar ominous movements were picked up by Israeli intelligence sources.

Then, suddenly, a Palestinian terrorist ambush of Soviet Jews headed through Austria for Israel made Kissinger jittery. He expressed great concern that the Israeli government—outraged and frustrated at the Austrian chancellor's capitulation to the terrorists' demand that in return for releasing the hostages Austria close some facilities it had made available to transiting Jewish emigrés—might retaliate by attacking Palestinian camps throughout the Arab Middle East. This, Kissinger feared, could set off a cycle of violence that could expand quickly into all-out war; and he warned the Israeli ambassador of the consequences.

As reports poured in on the intense military posturing now being undertaken by the potential belligerents, Kissinger feared, above all, a major Israeli preemptive strike, in the mode of its lightening raids at the outset of the 1967 war, to hobble the Syrian and Egyptian war machines; and he admonished Israeli officials to resist this temptation. The Secretary of State still refused to believe that Egypt and its allies might be planning to start a war as a deliberate act of policy. Even when Kissinger was informed on the night of October 4 that Russian dependents were being evacuated from Cairo and Damascus, he preferred to interpret the event as perhaps another indication of difficulties between the Soviets and their Arab hosts. His intelligence advisers, while disagreeing with this interpretation, still were not ready to predict war.

During the forty-eight hours preceding hostilities, with evidence from various sources confirming that the Syrian and Egyptian forward armored units were swinging into offensive formations, Kissinger personally phoned foreign minister Abba Eban to counsel him against an Israeli preemption. The American ambassador to Israel, Kenneth Keating, underscored Kissinger's views, warning his hosts that only if there was irrefutable proof that the Arabs were the aggressors would the United States consider itself morally obligated to help the Israelis. The implication was clear: If Israel struck a preemptive blow, it would have to fight alone.[26]

The continuing U.S. remonstrations against Israel's striking preemptively this time evidently worked. Against the advice of the Israeli Chief of Staff, Prime Minister Meir decided to allow her country to accept the first blows. The Arabs struck massively and simultaneously from Syria in the north and Egypt in the south on Yom Kippur morning, October 6, while many Israelis were attending religious services. It was a well-planned, well-coordinated, and efficiently executed attack.

The immediate physical losses suffered by Israel for letting the

Arabs strike first were large; but the ultimate gain was presumably of larger significance: namely, a clear moral claim on the United States for support of Israel as a victim of aggression. As it turned out, however, this moral claim had less currency in the White House than the Israelis had been led to believe.

The U.S. leaders, as should have been expected, would always put their own priorities first, and the resumption of hostilities once again made it plain that these were (a) to avoid a major war between the United States and the Soviet Union; (b) to ensure the survival of Israel (Nixon's and Kissinger's sentiments apart, they knew that it would be political suicide to allow Israel to be destroyed); (c) to prevent the Soviet Union from exploiting the conflict to enlarge its influence in the Middle East; and (d) to conduct U.S. diplomacy in the region in such a way as to enhance the regional and global prestige of the United States and to increase domestic support for the Nixon administration. None of these interests required unequivocal U.S. support for Israel's war aims or the underwriting of its military strategy. Rather, Nixon and Kissinger, in reassessing the new situation brought about by the onset of war, seemed—to the shock and dismay of the Israelis—to be moving back to the evenhanded approach they had flirted with prior to the 1970 Jordanian crisis.

The White House made no public condemnation during the 1973 war of either the Arabs or the Soviet Union. Kissinger articulated the objective of U.S. crisis diplomacy as follows:

> First, to end hostilities as quickly as possible—but secondly, to end hostilities in a manner that would enable us to make a major contribution to removing the conditions that have produced four wars between Arabs and Israelis in the last 25 years.
>
> We were aware that there were many interested parties. There were, of course, the participants in the conflict—Egypt and Syria on the Arab side, aided by many other Arab countries; Israel on the other. There was the Soviet Union. There were the other permanent members of the Security Council. . . .
>
> It was our view that the United States could be most effective in both . . . tasks . . . if we conducted ourselves so that we could remain in permanent contact with all of these elements in the equation. . . .

> Our position is . . . that the conditions that produced this war were clearly intolerable to the Arab nations and that in a process of negotiations it will be necessary [for all sides] to make substantial concessions.
>
> The problem will be to relate the Arab concern for the sovereignty over territories to the Israeli concern for secure boundaries. . . .
>
> We will make a major effort to bring about a solution that is considered just by all parties.[27]

Another premise—not publicly articulated at the time—was that these objectives could not be attained if either side achieved a clear military victory in the hostilities. It was Kissinger's adherence to this premise at different stages in the crisis that made him look anti-Israeli to many Israelis and their friends and anti-Arab to many Arabs and their friends—not to mention the reputation he gained with many Americans for perfidy and duplicity. Indeed, much of Kissinger's most controversial behavior—his procrastination in moving military supplies to Israel, the timing of his demands for a cease-fire in place, his pressures on the Israelis to free the surrounded Egyptian Third Army, and his tough yet conciliatory handling of the Russians—would seem fickle, if not irrational, without this premise.[28]

The most detailed account of the considerations Kissinger brought to bear on the crucial decisions of the U.S. government during the 1973 war is provided by William Quandt. A member of the National Security Council staff, Quandt attended most of the Washington Special Action Group (WSAG) meetings that Kissinger used as the basic sounding-board for exploring and choosing among his options. (The October 1973 crisis was managed in detail by Kissinger on behalf of the President, who was increasingly preoccupied by his personal crisis over Watergate.)

According to Quandt, at the outbreak of hostilities Kissinger expected a short war in which Israel would prevail. He was worried, however, that if the Israelis once again began to humiliate the Arabs the Soviets would find it difficult to stay out. Urgent diplomatic initiatives therefore were required to ensure that a cease-fire was reestablished on the basis of the territorial status quo prevailing before October 6. The cooperation of the Soviets would be essential in getting the Arabs to return to the status quo ante, so it was of vital importance that the Soviets understand that the United States would not countenance any new Israeli territorial expansion. Accordingly, Nixon sent Brezhnev a letter urging mutual restraint and the convening of the UN Security Council, while Kissinger pressed the case with his counterparts in the Soviet Union, Egypt, and Israel for a cease-fire based on the status quo ante. Otherwise, however, the United States kept a low profile during the first few days of the war.

Egypt and Syria, with major military units still in the territory they wished to reconquer, were not ready to accede to the cease-fire proposal. Kissinger was confident, however, that once the tide of battle turned against the Arabs they would change their tune, especially if Israel began to cross the canal into Egypt and move beyond the Golan Heights in Syria.

Between the third and sixth days of the war, the WSAG's assessments of the military prospects changed. Israel was finding it difficult to turn back the Arab assault. Suffering heavy losses of aircraft, the Israelis urgently appealed for more American arms and were informed that additional shipments had been approved, including a number of Phantom jets that would soon be on their way. It became impossible to ascertain who was gaining the upper hand as the Israelis launched a smashing counteroffensive on the Syrian front and began bombing Damascus. Assad and Sadat were putting great pressure on King Hussein of Jordan to open up a third front against Israel.

Kissinger's response to the rapidly developing military situation was to call for a cease-fire *in place*. Golda Meir immediately refused this revised proposal, insisting that any cease-fire must be tied to the restoration of the territorial dispositions prevailing before Yom Kippur. Sadat was cool to the Kissinger proposal, demanding concrete Israeli commitments to relinquish all land captured in 1967 as the condition for a cease-fire. The Russians, while not rejecting the cease-fire, and indicating willingness to cooperate with the United States on the diplomatic front, now began a major airlift of arms to the Syrians.

The Israelis pressed their case for accelerated U.S. arms deliveries with greater persistence. Kissinger moved slowly in responding to the Israeli entreaties, citing Defense Department objections to a massive resupply effort.[29] Quandt reveals, however, that the temporizing on the Israeli arms requests was part of the considered Kissinger strategy of (a) not having the United States emerge as Israel's ally in opposition to the Arabs and (b) pressuring the Israelis to accept a cease-fire in place.

Meanwhile, the shifting fortunes of the belligerents in the war itself were producing a shift in their attitudes toward a cease-fire in place. To the Israelis, who were once again on the military offensive and hopeful of more than regaining their lost ground, the idea began to look more attractive, especially if its actual implementation could be delayed for a few days, while to the Arabs it began to look more and more like a trap. On October 12 the Israeli government, still bargaining hard for maximum assurances of American arms supplies, accepted the principle of a cease-fire in place. Now it was Sadat who was unequivocally opposed.

Kissinger and Nixon, frustrated by the Egyptian leader's rejection of a cease-fire in place and suspecting that the Soviets were encouraging him to dig in his heels, decided that the time had come to change the Soviet–Arab calculations of gains from allowing the war to continue. Nixon authorized an acceleration and expansion of the delivery of Phantoms and ordered the U.S. military to fly the aircraft and other equipment directly into Israel. The principal purpose was to demonstrate to Sadat and the Kremlin that any prolongation of the war could not possibly operate to the military advantage of the Arabs—despite the flow of Soviet arms, which the United States could easily match. Nor could it be to their political advantage, for it would make it more difficult for the United States to convince Israeli hawks that the Arabs were sincerely interested in an equitable peace. A collateral purpose undoubtedly was to show the Russians, once again, that they would only be embarrassed if they attempted unilaterally to change the balance of military power in the Middle East.

With the American airlift under way, the Israelis launched into their climactic hard-driving offensive on both fronts. The Syrians were decisively thrown off the Golan Heights and pushed back along the Damascus road. To the south the Israeli troops crossed over to the west bank of the Suez Canal in a maneuver designed to encircle the Egyptian troops still in the Sinai penninsula and cut off their line of retreat back over the canal into Egypt. In a matter of days, Israel was decisively in control of the military situation around its extended borders. Now it was the Russians who sent out anxious calls for a cease-fire.

Brezhnev invited Kissinger to come to Moscow for "urgent consultations." The moment for a cease-fire might have arrived. Kissinger's basic premise that it would be counterproductive for the Israelis to humiliate the Arabs had not altered. He left for Moscow on October 20 with his bargaining position strengthened by a presidential request to Congress for $2.2 billion in emergency military aid for Israel.

While en route to Moscow, however, Kissinger received the news of the momentous Saudi Arabian decision to embargo oil shipments to the United States. Not only were the relative bargaining weights on each side of the Arab–Israeli conflict changed thereby, but, as Kissinger was to discover in the months and years ahead, so was the overall world power equation out of which Kissinger had fashioned his realpolitik concepts.[30]

The Kissinger–Brezhnev meeting in Moscow on October 21 produced an agreed-upon superpower approach to an Arab–Israeli truce: a cease-fire resolution, to be presented to the UN Security Council, that would call for a simple cease-fire in place and negotiations between the parties; and an eventual peace conference, to be chaired by both the United States and the Soviet Union. In effect, the superpowers were agreeing to act jointly to compel their respective clients to stop the fighting.

Despite the Israeli government's protest that it was not adequately consulted, the United States joined the Soviet Union in presenting their agreed-upon text of a cease-fire resolution to the United Nations the very next morning. And after less than three hours' deliberation by the Security Council, Resolution 338 was adopted by a vote of 14 to 0 (China did not vote). The October 22 Resolution was a brief but specific statement:

> *The Security Council:*
>   1. *Calls upon* all parties to the present fighting to cease all firing and terminate all military activity immediately, no later than 12 hours after the moment of the adoption of this decision, in the positions they now occupy;
>   2. *Calls upon* the parties concerned to start immediately after the cease-fire the implementation of Security Council resolution 242 (1967) in all of its parts;
>   3. *Decides* that, immediately and concurrently with the cease-fire, negotiations start between the parties concerned under appropriate auspices aimed at establishing a just and durable peace in the Middle East.[31]

The parties stopped shooting six hours after the Security Council passed its resolution, but not without some arm twisting by both superpowers. Neither Israel nor Egypt was in a position to object too strongly. Israel was now in military control of more territory than before the war started, and thus was in a strong bargaining position. Egypt was reeling from the Israeli counteroffensive and would probably lose even more ground if a cease-fire were delayed any longer. Syria, too, recognized the new realities and accepted the cease-fire the next day.

Almost immediately after the formal cessation, however, there were charges and countercharges of violations of the truce. Who was responsible was of less concern to Kissinger, however, than the fact that the Israelis were exploiting the opportunity to extend their lines on the Egyptian side of the canal, putting them in a position to capture the city of Suez and completely encircle the 100,000-man Egyptian Third Army Corps.

The new Israeli military thrusts and their noose-tightening around the surrounded Egyptian Third Army precipitated a new crisis for Kissinger as the Soviets indicated an intention to intervene directly with their own forces to enforce the cease-fire. Kissinger's response—one of the most daring of his career—was to threaten counteraction against both the Israelis and the Russians. He would show the Russians that the United States could yet control the Israelis and that therefore Soviet intervention was unneccesary to prevent total humilitation of the Arabs; and he would show the Israelis (and the rest of the world) that the United States still had the will and the power to deter a direct Soviet intervention, but only if the Israelis themselves acted with reasonable restraint.

Kissinger's reasons for insisting on Israeli restraint went beyond the imperative of preventing Soviet intervention. Now, with the Arab oil embargo in effect, it was more than ever important for the United States to demonstrate the capacity to separate itself from the more extreme Israeli actions and to act as an honest broker in the region on behalf of an equitable peace. Accordingly, Kissinger had resolved to at least prevent the Israelis from strangling the Egyptian Third Army Corps, even before the Soviets threatened to intervene. Exactly how Kissinger coerced the Israelis has not been revealed, though the United States had many obvious sanctions at hand in its role as Israel's main military supplier. He is reported to have insisted that, at a minimum, the Israelis permit humanitarian convoys of food, water, and medical supplies to reach the surrounded Egyptian soldiers, and to have implied that if the Israelis attempted to prevent this the United States would itself convoy in the supplies.[32] And it is known that in frequent phone conversations with the Israelis during these days Kissinger, as the Kalbs put it, "cajoled, pressured, implored, warned, threatened, and pleaded" that Israel not destroy the Egyptian Third Corps and do more to demonstrate firm adherence to the cease-fire.[33]

The threat of Soviet intervention emerged obliquely. On October 24 President Sadat appealed to the United States and the Soviet Union to send a joint U.S.–Soviet peace-keeping force to police the cease-fire. Kissinger immediately rejected the idea. Soviet troops in the Middle East could only spell additional trouble, with or without a U.S. counterpresence. That night Ambassador Dobrynin phoned Kissinger with a "very urgent" message from Secretary General Brezhnev to President Nixon—so urgent, said Dobrynin, that he must read it over the phone to Kissinger. "Let us act together," said Brezhnev, and "urgently dispatch Soviet and American contingents to Egypt" in order to "compel the observance of the cease-fire without delay." The Soviet leader also went beyond the Sadat proposal with a threat that Nixon later described as the most serious to U.S.–Soviet relations since the Cuban missile crisis: "I will say it straight," Brezhnev warned, "that if you find it impossible to act together with us in this matter, we should be faced with the necessity urgently to consider the question of taking appropriate steps unilaterally. Israel cannot be allowed to get away with the violations."[34]

U.S. intelligence agencies meanwhile were picking up signs of Soviet military movements—"a plethora of indicators," according to Secretary of Defense Schlesinger, that Soviet airborne divisions in southern Russia and Hungary had been placed on alert. More Soviet ships had entered the Mediterranean, and some unconfirmed reports suggested that they might be carrying nuclear warheads for the missiles sent to Egypt earlier in the year.[35]

While unsure of what the Soviets were really up to—a symbolic show of resolve? a bluff? an actual deployment of major military units?—the administration acted swiftly to put the Kremlin on notice that any unilateral introduction of Soviet military force into the area at this time would risk a dangerous confrontation with the United States. All of the Nixon administration's principal national security advisers unanimously recommended that U.S. military forces around the world be placed visibly on alert at an intermediate DEFCON (defense condition) level, which meant that leaves would be canceled and most forces, including the Strategic Air Command, would be brought to a higher-than-normal state of readiness. The President concurred and so ordered, leaving the precise implementation up to the Secretary of Defense.[36] Nixon also asked Kissinger to develop a contingency plan for sending U.S. troops into the Middle East in the event that the Soviets were not deterred from intervening.[37]

Nixon held back on his verbal reply to Brezhnev until he was sure that the Soviets had picked up the first signs of the U.S. military alert, thereby ensuring that his words would have maximum psychological impact. While indicating some openness to the idea of having some American and Soviet noncombat personnel go into the area as part of an augmented UN observation team, the President categorically rejected "your proposal for a particular kind of action, that of sending Soviet and American military contingents to Egypt. It is clear," said Nixon, "that the forces necessary to impose the cease-fire terms on the two sides would be massive and would require the closest coordination so as to avoid bloodshed. This is not only clearly infeasible, but it is not appropriate to the situation." Moreover, warned the President, "you must know . . . that we could in no event accept unilateral action. . . . Such action would produce incalculable consequences which would be in the interest of neither of our countries and which would end all we have striven so hard to achieve."[38] In his October 25 press conference, Kissinger insisted that "we do not consider ourselves in a confrontation with the Soviet Union. We do not believe it is necessary, at this moment, to have a confrontation. In fact, we are prepared to work cooperatively [with them]. . . . But cooperative action precludes unilateral action, and the President decided that it was essential that we make clear our attitude toward unilateral steps."[39]

CBS correspondent Marvin Kalb asked the Secretary of State whether the American alert might have been prompted as much by American domestic requirements as by the diplomatic requirements of the Middle Eastern situation—implying that the Nixon administration, reeling from the Watergate affair, needed its own "missile crisis" to reestablish its prestige with the American electorate. Kissinger's response was angry and defensive: "We are attempting to conduct the foreign policy of the United States with regard for what we owe not to the electorate but to future generations. And it is a symptom of what is happening in our country that it could even be suggested that the United States would alert its forces for domestic reasons." He was absolutely confident, said Kissinger, that when the record was finally made available it would show that "the President had no other choice as a responsible national leader."[40]

An hour after Kissinger's press conference, the Soviet Union joined the United States and the other members of the Security Council in voting affirmatively for Resolution 340, demanding an immediate and complete cease-fire and a return to the positions occupied by the belligerents prior to the recent round of violations, and setting up a UN emergency force composed of non-permanent members of the Security Council (thus excluding the USSR and the United States) to oversee the cease-fire.[41] The guns fell silent on the Middle Eastern battlefields, and an intricate set of negotiations commenced to separate the forces, return prisoners of war, establish enforceable truce zones, and begin the long process toward an agreed-upon settlement of the underlying Arab–Israeli conflict.

Historians will long debate whether Kissinger played his cards with consummate skill or whether he (and the world) were miraculously lucky to avoid World War III. Kissinger did, however, establish convincingly that he was neither pro-Israeli nor pro-Arab but genuinely of the conviction that vital U.S. interests required a durable Middle Eastern peace, and that this had to be based on specific political arrangements acceptable to all parties plus a local military equilibrium. This now-secured reputation served him well in the activist-mediator role that became the essence of his subsequent Middle East diplomacy.

Kissinger's New Middle East Diplomacy

The brink of war, like the hangman's noose, disciplines the statesman's mind. Out of his practical experience in terminating the 1973 war, more than out of his realpolitik concepts, Kissinger finally put together a sophisticated Middle East policy for the United States that corresponded more closely to the complexity and volatility of the area than the administration's diplomacy following the Jordan crisis.

The code term for Kissinger's new Middle East diplomacy became "step by step"—a reference to Kissinger's method of getting (a) Egypt and Israel to disengage their forces in January 1974 from the dangerous overlapping dispositions in which they were left at the cease-fire the previous October; (b) getting Syria and Israel to reestablish a narrow demilitarized buffer zone between them in May 1974; and (c) getting Egypt and Israel to agree in September 1975 to the so-called Sinai II disengagement, which provided for the first substantial relinquishment by Israel of part of the territory it had conquered in the 1967 war, a thick demilitarized buffer zone comprising most of the relinquished territory, to be policed by the United Nations and a special observer team of U.S. civilians, as well as some limited Egyptian indicators of Israel's legitimacy, such as the allowance of nonmilitary cargoes bound for Israel to pass through the Suez Canal.

The step-by-step method separated tangible specific issues, on which there were incentives to achieve immediate agreement, from the larger issues in the Arab–Israeli conflict, which still generated high emotion on both sides. Rather than being asked to agree on a comprehensive set of principles for the settlement at the end of the road as the basis for the immediate specific negotiations, the parties would be induced to start down the road without an agreed-upon picture of their destination any more specific than the highly ambiguous UN Resolution 242. The process of working out an agreement, even on relatively minor matters, would have a salutary effect on the negotiating climate farther down the road. At every step vested interests would be built up on each side, which would not want to see the disintegration of what had already been achieved and therefore would act as a voice of moderation, possibly a peace lobby, for that side.

The step-by-step approach, however, could not be sustained for long if either side began to regard it as a ruse to prevent the attainment of highly valued objectives. This, indeed, soon emerged as a large problem for Sadat, who had to defend himself against militants in his own country and throughout the Arab world—especially against the Palestinians, who charged that he was selling out the goal of regaining the lost Arab territories in order to buy peace with Israel and the good will of the United States. As time went on, therefore, Kissinger was compelled to increase his pressure on the Israelis to make sufficiently meaningful concessions for Sadat to be able to demonstrate to his militant critics that substantial and rapid progress was being made toward the main Arab goal.

Another feature of the matured Kissinger diplomacy was to treat the Arab world not as "the other side" in the Arab–Israeli conflict but as a highly differentiated set of countries with which it was more productive to deal bilaterally on most issues, including relations with Israel. Even categorizing them into moderates and militants was too neat; and acting if such a division were valid might mean neglecting opportunities for the United States to build special lines of influence with each of the countries. Thus, Syria and Iraq, the leaders of the so-called militants, had their own historical enmities and divergent attitudes toward the Christian–Muslim conflict in Lebanon; and Egypt, Jordan, and Saudi Arabia, leaders of the so-called moderates, had played vastly different parts in the cold war, with Egypt becoming a Soviet client and maintaining a professedly "progressive" regime while the Jordanian and Saudi monarchies built their armed forces around American-supplied equipment. Then again, Saudi Arabia, which along with Iran was a dominant force in the oil producer cartel, was in a different class from Egypt and Jordan when it came to bargaining with the United States and other industrialized countries. Moreover, each of these countries had its own problems with displaced Palestinians and a different set of preferences and priorities when it came to the demands of the various Palestinian guerrilla organizations against Israel.

Of course, if U.S. bilateral diplomacy was conducted crudely, the various Arab countries might see it as a divide-and-rule policy designed to advance Israeli interests and might join to present a united front even if such unity would contradict important national interests. Even the subtle Kissinger found it impossible to sustain the bilateral approach, which involved frequent "shuttling" between the principal Middle Eastern capitals, without creating suspicion that he was playing off one country against another. To mollify such suspicions, especially near the end of his tenure, he began to weave a tangle of complicated reassurances, often in the form of promises of special economic and military-supply relationships, not all of which were likely to be backed up by the Congress and some of which required him to make compensatory promises to Israel.

A corollary to the strategy of building multiple relationships in the Middle East was a somewhat more relaxed attitude toward the Soviet role in the region than Kissinger had shown when he promised to "expel" the Soviets from Egypt. If it was now deemed counterproductive to polarize the Arabs into moderate and militant camps, it was even more disadvantageous, from a global geopolitical perspective, to overlay this with pro-Soviet and pro-U.S. groupings. This simply would give the Russians too many automatic clients. It should not be because of U.S. policy that countries ran to the arms of the Soviet Union or were reluctant to come to the United States to satisfy needs that were not adequately attended to by the Russians. The evolution of Sadat's policy should serve as a model: Let events run their natural course and Arab nationalism would assert itself against Soviet imperialism. The process might not take this course, however, if the United States acted as if it were illegitimate for Middle Eastern countries to have "peace and friendship" treaties or client–patron relationships with the USSR, or as if in order to build a relationship with the United States one must renounce relations with Moscow; for such an uncompromising U.S. policy would itself cut against the grain of local nationalism and pride, and might only further alienate some of these countries from the United States.

The more permissive U.S. attitude toward a Soviet Middle Eastern presence, however, might have its own pitfalls, particularly where the easiest way for the Russians to get a local foothold is through supplying military equipment. Increased flows of Soviet arms into the area might produce adverse shifts in the local power balance, which the United States might need to counter by further military buildups of Israel and/or other primary U.S. clients. Thus, what started out as a relaxed approach could result in a new spiral of competitive arming of military clients and even a rigid repolarization of the area.

In short, the new Kissinger strategy of defusing immediately combustible situations and weaving a web of positive relations with virtually all states in the region (regardless of their attitudes toward Israel) might not be sufficient to (a) prevent the expansion of Soviet imperialism in the Middle East, (b) reduce the prospects of a war between the superpowers starting in the region, and (c) ensure the continued survival of Israel. Moreover, the strategy could boomerang, resulting in another Arab–Israeli war with higher levels of armaments on both sides and with the Russians more ensconced in the area than ever; and unless in the interim the industrial world substantially reversed its growing dependence on Middle Eastern oil, the United States, Western Europe, and Japan might be severely divided among themselves and troubled by internal political dissension over the costs and risks of coming to Israel's assistance during its period of maximum peril.

Kissinger must have known, on the basis of his past historical studies and his baptism in the fire of Middle Eastern politics, that symptomatic fire-fighting and step-by-step conflict resolution techniques were only surface ameliorants. If any region in the world required a "structure of peace" to prevent events there from severely undermining U.S. external security and internal stability, it was the Middle East. Kissinger had reestablished American competence in the area, but something more was required. Perhaps he had a grand design, some architecture, a "vision"; but this remained unarticulated and could not be inferred from his behavior.

5

THE ANACHRONISM OF CONSERVATIVE REALPOLITIK

> In each period there exist anachronisms, states which appear backward and even decadent to those who fail to realize they are dealing with the most tenacious remnant of a disintegrating world order.
> Henry A. Kissinger, in *A World Restored: The Politics of Conservatism in a Revolutionary Age**

The evolution of U.S. crisis diplomacy in the Middle East from 1969 to 1976 reflected the more general metamorphosis in U.S. foreign policy over which Henry Kissinger presided. What was once viewed as a protracted conflict between the forces of radicalism, revolution, and chaos (exploited by the Soviet Union) and the forces of moderation, stability, and order (led by the United States) showed itself to be a more complicated and many-sided interaction of ideological and material forces in which the natural and most effective role of the United States might often be that of sponsor of progressive reform. Similarly, the traditional stabilizing mechanism available to those who wanted to preserve the status quo—an advantageous balance of military power—was often insufficient for containing the forces of chaos and frequently inappropriate as a means through which the United States could exert influence on the side of constructive change.

The metamorphosis in U.S. policy was hardly smooth, how-

---

* Grosset's Universal Library, 1964, p. 212.

ever, and often found the Nixon and Ford administrations falling back on conservative realpolitik concepts and stances.

• Nixon and Kissinger discounted the humanitarian and moral implications of Pakistani President Yahya Khan's brutal suppression of the Bangladesh independence movement in 1971. They stressed rather the "illegitimacy" of India's reactive intervention and attempt to "dismember" the sovereign state of Pakistan. Reversing the standing U.S. policy of scrupulously avoiding taking sides in India–Pakistan conflicts, the administration aligned itself diplomatically with Pakistan in the Bangladesh conflict, threatened to call off the Nixon–Brezhnev summit scheduled for the spring of 1972 if the Kremlin did not put restraining pressure on India, and dispatched a Marine intervention task force, ostentatiously escorted by the nuclear aircraft carrier *Enterprise*, into the Bay of Bengal. This was a symbolic show of force, apparently with no real intention to directly participate in the fight. The administration was most worried that a decisive Indian victory over Pakistan (China's diplomatic ally in its own border conflicts with India), with the United States standing idly by, would destabilize the Asian balance of power—now viewed as a subordinate level of the triangular U.S.–Soviet–Chinese balance. As it turned out, the Indians prevailed in effecting the separation of Bangladesh from East Pakistan despite the U.S. action. Nevertheless, Nixon and Kissinger claimed success in deterring India from pressing its advantage to the point of militarily attacking West Pakistan and occupying Pakistani-claimed areas of Kashmir.

• In authorizing covert CIA programs to support Chilean opponents of the Marxist regime of Salvador Allende Gossens, and implicating the United States at least indirectly in the violent military ouster and death of Allende in September 1973, Nixon and Kissinger re-embraced the ideological anticommunist definitions of U.S. interests that they claimed to be discarding in their "structure of peace" concepts. (Kissinger himself had often ridiculed claims by the U.S. military that Chile had vital strategic importance, and is reputed to be the originator of the quip that a communist Chile would be a dagger pointed at the heart of Tierra del Fuego.)

• Kissinger's policy of politically quarantining Portugal—of acting as if that country had a contagious disease during the seventeen months of political turmoil following the April 1974 reformist coup in Lisbon—had the ostensible geopolitical ratio-nale of insulating NATO military organs, especially the Nuclear Planning Group, from possible subversion by Portuguese left-ists. The ruling cabinet of the provisional government, although led by a popular general and a prominent liberal, included two leaders of the Portuguese Communist party as well as several so-cialists. Actually, it was rather easy for the NATO organization to protect its essential functions against communist subversion by setting up special subcommittees, excluding Portugal, to deal with sensitive matters. Kissinger's fears apparently went deeper: a communist victory in Portugal would profoundly destabilize the European equilibrium, providing the Soviet Union for the first time with a major presence in Western Europe and on the strategically located Iberian peninsula. (The Portuguese commu-nists, under Alvaro Cunhal, were openly pro-Soviet and not part of the liberalizing "Eurocommunist" movement.) Accordingly, as the communists intensified their efforts to take over the central and local governing apparatus of Portugal, Kissinger made it known that he intended to subject that country to virtually com-plete diplomatic and economic isolation from the West unless the Portuguese socialists and liberals expelled the communists from official positions of influence in Lisbon. Noncommunist leaders in Portugal, the U.S. ambassador in Lisbon, and some of America's European allies tried to dissuade Kissinger from such a coercive approach, arguing that it would only gain the commu-nists greater sympathy among the Portuguese people. (Kis-singer's coercive diplomacy was never really put to the test. Cunhal impatiently overplayed his hand by attemping a military *putsch*. This rash communist bid for total power was defeated by a coalition of moderate military officers and democratic social-ists, who now had sufficient grounds of their own for denying the communists important positions in the government.)

• Kissinger's response to the phenomenon of "Eurocom-munism" was also a product of a persisting cold war mind set. Kissinger was mistrustful of pledges by communist party leaders in Italy, France, and Spain to respect freedom of expression and association and democratic political processes, including the rights of opposition parties to openly oppose a communist-controlled government and the obligation of governments to turn over power to other parties when the electorate so decides. He regarded such pledges as a deceptive strategem to undercut the reluctance of the noncommunist parties in Western Europe to form electoral alliances and coalition governments with the communists. Once the communists were allowed to share power, argued Kissinger, they would have no scruples about reneging on their promises and, like the communists in Eastern Europe in the late 1940s, would decisively suppress all opposition parties and deal brutally with anyone who cried foul. Moreover, the Western hope that, once in power, the European communist parties would remain nationalist and pursue international policies distinct from those of the Soviet Union was regarded by Kissinger as a dangerously naive basis for currently relaxing the barriers to their attaining power. It would be damaging enough, from Kissinger's viewpoint, if any of the key NATO countries turned initially neutralist. His strategy, therefore, was to allude openly to the international economic and political costs that would be incurred by any Western European country that turned toward communism—a drying up of foreign investments of private capital, and second-class status in or expulsion from NATO—as a deterrent to any power-sharing experiments with the Eurocommunists.

• Kissinger's vacillation and delay in responding to the July 1974 Greek nationalist coup in Cyprus that deposed Archbishop Makarios was perhaps attributable in part to the Secretary of State's preoccupation with the Middle East crisis and the climactic traumas of Watergate. But the fact that, when preoccupied, Kissinger gave the benefit of the doubt to the Greek military junta that engineered the coup, and then remained aloof as Turkey, using U.S. arms in violation of congressional restrictions, invaded Cyprus to protect the island's Turkish minority, was revealing of his natural, almost instinctual, biases: suspicion, even contempt, of democratic reformers and populist politicans (into which category he placed Archbishop Makarios) and faith in the reliability of decisive, militaristic, disciplined leaders such as might be found in a Greek military junta or in NATO-loyal Turkish governments.

• In May 1975, two weeks after the final communist takeover of Saigon, U.S. marines stormed a Cambodian communist stronghold on Tang Island in the Gulf of Siam to rescue the American crewmen from the freighter *Mayaguez*, which had been seized for penetrating what Cambodia claimed to be its territorial waters. Fighter planes from the U.S aircraft carrier *Coral Sea* bombed the Cambodian mainland. In this swift use of force, Kissinger and President Ford impatiently preempted their own diplomatic initiatives through the UN and neutral channels. They found out afterwards that the Cambodian government had decided to release the crew before the marine and air assault had started. If that information had been in Ford's hands, the lives of the thirty-eight Americans who died in the operation, not to mention the larger number of Cambodians, could have been saved. But Kissinger and Ford, having just shown themselves unable to prevent the communists from attaining total military victory in Vietnam in violation of the Paris agreements of 1973, apparently were particularly anxious to demonstrate that the United States, under their leadership, was still not to be trifled with. By seizing the *Mayaguez*, puny Cambodia provided them with the opportunity for a show of the old machismo without the risk of major war.

The Crisis in the World Economic Order

The destabilization of international economic relations that resulted from the oil price increases and embargo imposed by oil-exporting countries in 1973 and 1974 was initially perceived and responded to by Kissinger mainly as an element in the East–West balance of power and as a critical variable in the Arab–Israeli conflict. To the extent that he regarded the economic and political actions of the Organization of Petroleum Exporting

Countries (OPEC) as serious threats worthy of his attention, it was insofar as (a) the denial of oil to the Western industrialized nations or Japan might bring about the economic and political collapse of key members of the anticommunist alliance, and (b) the Arab members of OPEC, using such a denial threat, could coerce the industrialized nations into supporting the Arab side in the Arab–Israeli conflict. The emergence of these threats in connection with the Arab–Israeli war of 1973 riveted Kissinger's attention on the economics as well as the politics of the global energy situation and, because the energy situation was now so closely linked with the overall workings of the international economy, compelled him to quickly educate himself on the structure and condition of the world economic order. What he found significantly complicated his views on geopolitics and effected a transformation in his statesmanship. Global equilibrium, the structure of peace, the security of the United States itself—all of these depended as much on the distribution of economic power as on the distribution of military power and the pattern of political loyalties. It was therefore part of the art of high statesmanship to be able to manipulate the international economic variables, not simply as adjuncts to U.S.–Soviet détente but as elements in the very essence of international power.

In this field, too, it was in responding to crisis situations that Kissinger was able to seize the reins and perform most effectively while others were confused and demoralized. But during the first Nixon administration (1969–1972) the driver's seat for U.S. foreign economic policy was usually occupied by Secretary of the Treasury John Connally or the President himself.

The U.S. domestic economy was in deep trouble in 1971—"stagflation," it was called—in ways that could have damaging effects on Nixon's chances for reelection: unemployment was dangerously high, simultaneously with abnormally high increases in the prices of goods and services. U.S. labor unions had turned protectionist, arguing that a large part of the unemployment problem was due to the influx of foreign goods produced by cheap foreign labor, sometimes in foreign subsidiaries of U.S. multinational corporations. Trade and monetary experts were alarmed at the rapidly deteriorating U.S. balance of international payments, reflecting the lag of U.S. exports behind imports and the increasing outflow of U.S. dollars in the form of overseas investments. Monetarists claimed that the dollar was highly overvalued in relation to other currencies and that this was dangerous for the health of the U.S. economy; it artifically made U.S. goods more expensive than they should be on the world market, and made foreign goods cheaper in the United States. There was growing pressure in international financial circles for the United States to devalue the dollar, but this would mean that the domestic economy would have to absorb the first shocks of the international readjustment; moreover, such talk could cause a dangerous collapse of the whole monetary system as holders of U.S. dollars—the basic and most widely held of all currencies—rushed to cash them in for other currencies or, worse yet, demanded that the United States exchange their dollars for gold at the preestablished price of $35 per ounce. (There was nowhere near that amount of gold in the U.S. Treasury.)

Under these circumstances, argued Secretary of the Treasury Connally, the United States should begin to insist that others in the system assume some of the burdens of making the international economy work. The West Europeans and the Japanese, having recovered from World War II to become major competitors of the United States, should no longer be babied. Speaking in Munich in May 1971, Connally bluntly told the Europeans that the United States was losing patience with the other industrialized nations, which it was still protecting in the NATO alliance, for not pulling their weight in the economic system. Questions were beginning to arise in the United States, he warned, over how the costs of NATO and other mutual security arrangements should be allocated. "I find it an impressive fact, and a depressing fact, that the persisting underlying balance of payments deficit which causes so much concern, is more than covered, year in and year out, by our net military expenditures abroad." Financing the free world's military shield was part of the burden of leadership that the United States should not cast off, said the Treasury Secretary, *but*

> the comfortable assumption that the United States should—in the broader political interests of the free world—be willing to bear disproportionate economic costs does not fit the facts of today. I do not for a moment call into question the worth of a self-confident, cohesive Common Market, a strong Japan, and a progressing Canada, to the peace and prosperity of the free world community.
>
> The question is only—but the only is important—whether those nations, now more than amply supplied with [financial] reserves as well as productive power, should not now be called upon for fresh initiatives in opening their markets to the products of others. . . .
>
> No longer does the U.S. economy dominate the free world. No longer can considerations of friendship, or need, or capacity justify the United States' carrying so heavy a share of the common burdens.
>
> And, to be perfectly frank, no longer will the American people permit their government to engage in international actions in which the true long-run interests of the U.S. are not just as clearly recognized as those of the nations with which we deal.[1]

Ten weeks after Connally delivered this stern lecture, President Nixon announced a "new economic policy" to "blaze the trail to a new prosperity." In addition to domestic measures to create new jobs (mainly tax breaks for industry to stimulate investment in new plants), to stimulate more consumer demand (a repeal of the 7 percent excise tax on automobiles and an increase in personal income tax deductions for dependents), and to control inflation (a temporary freeze on all wages and prices throughout the United States), Nixon ordered a set of measures designed to coerce the other industrialized nations into reconsidering their reluctance to allow the United States to openly compete with them in the international economy.

On the advice of Secretary Connally, he temporarily suspended the convertibility of the dollar into gold or other international reserve assets. This technical action, dubbed by journalists as "slamming the U.S. gold window," was taken, the President explained, to prevent the international money speculators from "waging an all-out war against the American dollar." Also on the advice of Connally, Nixon imposed a temporary tax of 10 percent on goods imported into the United States. This action was taken, he said, "to make certain that American products will not be at a disadvantage because of unfair [currency] exchange rates. When the unfair treatment is ended, the import tax will end as well." Now that the other nations have regained their vitality and have become our competitors, argued Nixon, "the time has come for them to bear their fair share of defending freedom around the world" and maintaining a stable international economic order.

> The time has come for exchange rates to be set straight and for the major nations to compete as equals. There is no longer any need for the United States to compete with one hand tied behind her back.[2]

The European allies of the United States and Japan were shocked at Nixon's harsh tone and uncompromising posture. Kissinger and Nixon both had criticized the Kennedy and Johnson administrations for their arrogant unilateralism on matters of concern to the alliance and had pledged a more consultative approach. Now Washington, without prior consultation, not only was taking it upon itself to change key structural elements in the international monetary system but also was unilaterally imposing a special tariff (the 10 percent "import surcharge") on goods from its trading partners—in effect, twisting their arms until they gave in to U.S. demands to revalue their currencies.

The damaging effects of such coercive unilateralism to an overall system of mutual accountability among the economically advanced noncommunist countries alarmed the chairman of the Council on International Economic Policy, Peter Peterson, who implored Kissinger to intervene with Nixon against Connally's Texan shoot-it-out style. Kissinger, although almost totally preoccupied with Vietnam, and still unfamiliar with the intricacies of international economics, nonetheless weighed in in behalf of a less confrontationist approach.[3]

Nixon softened the U.S. position somewhat in subsequent negotiations with the Europeans and the Japanese by agreeing to devalue the U.S. dollar as the others up-valued their currencies. The result was the agreement concluded at the December 1971 meeting of the International Monetary Fund (IMF) to realign all major currencies and subsequently allow them to "float," that is, to have their values set by supply and demand on the world money markets within rather broad margins. Collaterally, the European Economic Community agreed to a new round of extensive trade negotiations with the United States. Japan also exhibited a cooperative attitude in implementing the "voluntary" restraints on its exports to the United States and the import barrier liberalizations it had accepted earlier in the year in exchange for U.S. cooperation in returning Okinawa.

The official tone of mutual accommodation surrounding the December 1971 meeting of the IMF was capped by Nixon's personal appearance at the meeting to bless what he termed "the most significant monetary agreement in the history of the world." But this could not erase the fact that the United States had used not only economic coercion but also hints of a withdrawal of military protection to compel its allies to accede to its desires.

If the international system was now to feature intense competition and coercive bargaining within the anticommunist alliance as well as East–West rivalry, America's partners would make their own adjustments to this new reality. Perhaps General de Gaulle was right after all, and Europe (and even Japan) would have to seek a unique role in the system that would maximize its bargaining advantages vis-à-vis both superpowers. Kissinger would reap the bitter harvest of the seeds won in 1971 when, at the conclusion of the Vietnam war two years later, he turned his attention to the disintegrating "Atlantic community." The potentially disastrous geopolitical implications of the disintegrative trends would be driven home during the Yom Kippur war, when he tried to obtain allied cooperation against Arab oil blackmail and Soviet military threats.

By 1973 the differences in membership and purposes between the North Atlantic security community on the one hand and the

West European economic community on the other hand were prominently exposed and crucially affecting relations between the United States and Europe. With the new era of détente reducing the immediacy of the common-defense purposes of NATO, the principle that everyone should do his part for the good of the whole was difficult to enforce. Those with the greatest military power did not automatically exercise the greatest authority, and conflicts within the community were harder to resolve than previously. Where nonmilitary matters were at issue—trade barriers, currency exchange rates, the terms of technological cooperation, access to energy supplies, environmental controls—there was now more opportunity for special-interest groups to press their demands on their own governments and on the deliberative assemblies and bureaucracies of the European and Atlantic communities. Even when it came to military issues, such as determining the size, composition, and strategy of NATO forces, the debates were less over how best to defend against military attack from the East than over the distribution of the economic burdens of alliance membership. Previously, when the United States had insisted that the economically thriving NATO countries provide more for their own defense and purchase military equipment from the United States to offset the U.S. balance-of-payments costs of American forces in Europe, it had been easier to compel agreement on the basis of the overriding imperatives of mutual security. But as the question of sharing military burdens became linked to monetary and trade issues (as had been done by Nixon and Connally in 1971), the United States found itself bargaining against a coalition of European countries in NATO.[4]

Against this background Kissinger proclaimed his "Year of Europe" in an address before Associated Press editors meeting in New York City on April 23, 1973. The formulation was remarkably patronizing, leading French wags to complain that it was as if an inconstant husband had suddenly announced a "year of the wife." Smarting from the insensitive and indifferent treatment they had been getting from top officials of the Nixon administration, European governments were predisposed to read the worst implications into the appeal for transatlantic cooperation, which Kissinger had meant as a sincere offer to make amends. His ringing call for a "new Atlantic charter" that would "strike a new balance between self-interest and the common interest, . . . identify interests and positive values beyond security in order to engage once again the commitment of people and parliaments, . . . [and set forth] a shared view of the world we seek to build" was received skeptically by the Europeans. They read his indelicately phrased observation—"The United States has global interests and responsibilities. Our European allies have regional interests"—as a reassertion of the hegemonic conceit that the United States had an obligation to consult with the Europeans only on specifically European matters but that the Europeans should consult with their superpower protector on all matters of significance. And they squirmed uncomfortably at the unintended irony of a Nixon administration official preaching to them that "we cannot hold together if each country or region asserts its autonomy whenever it is to its benefit and invokes unity to curtail the independence of others."[5]

As a realist, Kissinger understood the inevitability of such tensions, given the centrifugal forces pulling the international system away from the bipolar abnormalities of the early cold war period and back toward a more normal pattern of multiple and shifting coalitions. He was disappointed at the cool European response to his call for a new Atlantic charter, but not terribly surprised. Yet he still hoped that in times of profound challenge to their common values from the Soviet Union or some other source, at least the NATO nations would bond together to protect Western civilization. He was therefore deeply dismayed at the Europeans' failure to rally around the alliance leader in the fall of 1973, when the very fabric of society was threatened by OPEC's quadrupling of the price of oil and the extortionist embargo imposed by the Arabs on oil exports to Israel's supporters. Not only did France, Britain, and Japan, in conducting their own bilateral negotiations with the Arab producers, undermine Kissinger's efforts to organize a united front of the major consumer nations to break the producer cartel, but some of the NATO countries were so anxious to disassociate themselves from actions in support of Israel that they refused to allow U.S. planes to use their bases or even to overfly their territory to transport military supplies to Israel during the 1973 war. The American Secretary of State regarded such weakness in the face of Arab pressure as spineless and craven, reminiscent of the way European governments caved in to Hitler's demands on the eve of World War II.

Kissinger was able to adapt to this reality too, recognizing that the European and Japanese economies were more vulnerable to price changes and limited oil supplies than the United States, and that the Europeans had developed considerable experience, still lacking in the United States, in diplomatic dealings with the Arabs and other Third World raw materials producers on such matters. He also had to recognize how little he knew about the economic side of the world energy situation, and accordingly he quickly recast his staff to give it intense study and began personally to avail himself of governmental and nongovernmental counsel on the subject. This crash self-improvement course was paralleled by a series of urgent consultations with the major oil-consuming countries and with representatives of the producer countries so that, upon the termination of the Arab–Israeli war and the lifting of the oil embargo, the United States would be ready to propose a set of international rules for a rational and fair commerce in this vital resource. Failure to resolve the energy problem on the basis of international cooperation, Kissinger warned, would threaten the world with a vicious cycle of competition, autarchy, rivalry, and depression such as had led to the collapse of world order in the 1930s.

The basic approach to the energy problem that Kissinger would follow during the rest of his tenure as Secretary of State was presented by him in broad outline to a conference of major oil-consuming countries summoned by the United States in February 1974:

    1. *Conservation.* Kissinger called for a "new energy ethic" designed to promote the conservation and efficient use of

energy supplies by all countries. The United States, being the world's most profligate country, bore a special responsibility in this regard, admitted Kissinger, and he pledged an expansion of this country's crisis-stimulated conservation measures and offered to collaborate in a mutual review by the energy-consuming countries of one another's programs.

2. *Alternate fossil energy sources.* Sources neglected during the era of low-cost oil now needed to be exploited—coal, of course, but also shale and offshore oil. The United States would be ready to coordinate its programs of new exploration and exploitation with the other consumer countries, and this might involve multilateral efforts to encourage the flow of private capital into new industries for producing energy, as well as governmental arrangements to accelerate the search for new energy sources.

3. *Research and development.* The United States was prepared, said Kissinger, "to make a major contribution of its most advanced energy research and development [technologies] to a broad program of international cooperation," including technologies to promote the use of nuclear reactors under controls to prevent the spread of nuclear weapons.

4. *Emergency sharing of petroleum.* The most generous of the Kissinger proposals, but also the most problematic in view of likely opposition in Congress, was his offer "to share available energy in times of emergency or prolonged shortages. We would be prepared to allocate an agreed portion of our total petroleum supply provided other consuming countries with indigenous production do likewise."

5. *International financial cooperation.* New international measures, but above all a spirit of international responsibility, were needed to cope with the accumulation of petrodollars and their "recycling" back into the consumer countries. These measures, said Kissinger, should include "steps to facilitate the fuller participation of producing nations in existing international institutions and to contribute to the urgent needs of the developing countries."

Our ultimate goal, according to America's arch practitioner and conceptualizer of conservative realpolitik, must be

> to create a cooperative framework within which producers and consumers will be able to accommodate their differences and reconcile their needs and aspirations. Only in this way can we assure the evolution and growth of the world economy and the stability of international relations. We must work toward the objective of preventing coercion of the weak by the strong and of the strong by the weak. . . .
>
> As we look toward the end of this century we know that the energy crisis indicates the birth pains of global interdependence. Our response could well determine our capacity to deal with the international agenda of the future.
>
> We confront a fundamental decision. Will we consume ourselves in nationalistic rivalry which the realities of interdependence make suicidal? Or will we acknowledge our interdependence and shape cooperative solutions?[6]

During the next twenty months, the Secretary of State devoted much of his and his staff's talents to the intricate diplomatic and planning tasks of fleshing out the broad framework and giving concrete reality to this visionary rhetoric. This was not simply posturing. Kissinger understood that the essence of statesmanship in the emerging international system was the ability to deal with the politics of economics and technology. He who had once dubbed such matters the province of second-rate minds now seemed to relish demonstrating his mastery of his new specialty. Confidently embodying a synthesis of finance minister and geopolitician, he grabbed the international ball back from the departments of Treasury and Commerce and made it clear once again to foreign governments that the President's principal adviser and spokesman on all matters of foreign policy—including economics—was Henry Kissinger.

This was a more complicated policy arena than Kissinger had written about or operated in during his first four years as a high government official. At home there were more players in the multiple legislative and bureaucratic games in the field of foreign economic policy making than there were in the field of national security policy and U.S.–Soviet relations. Kissinger was to find that the commanding position of the United States in the global economy was not readily cashed in for bargaining chips on the specific issues he wanted to deal with.

Even when the United States was a leading producer of goods for which there was high international demand, such as high technology and food, the international free market principles to which the United States was officially committed, combined with the opposition of domestic sellers to export controls, blocked Kissinger's efforts to convert these assets into flexible instruments of diplomacy. Kissinger flirted with using the position of the United States as the largest exporter of food grains to exert leverage against the oil producer cartel. But paradoxically, the 1974–1975 famine conditions in India and the African Sahel removed this option. For to hold back food from the international market at a time of vast starvation, and by so doing further drive up world prices, would be regarded as an act of the grossest cruelty. Kissinger was resourceful, however, in turning U.S. dominance as a food producer into more general world political leadership by proposing a World Food Conference and, at its meeting in Rome in November 1974, offering a comprehensive scheme for nationally held but internationally coordinated stocks of surplus grain to stabilize grain prices and help the countries with the greatest need.[7]

Still, Kissinger's lack of tangible and effective leverage against the energy producers continued to bother him, and he found it hard to resist the temptation to reach for the familiar political–military bargaining chips.

At the end of 1974, Kissinger, unsuccessful in his effort to form a solid consensus among the major consumer countries for bargaining with OPEC, allowed himself to be quoted in *Business Week* on the pitfalls, but also the possibilities, of political and military power plays against the Arab oil producers. The only way to bring oil prices down immediately in the absence of consumer solidarity, Kissinger told his interviewers, would be to "create a political crisis of the first magnitude." When probed to describe what he meant, Kissinger talked of massive political warfare against countries like Saudi Arabia and Iran to make them risk their political stability and maybe their security if they do not cooperate. That is too high a price to pay even for an immediate reduction in oil prices.

If you bring about an overthrow of the existing system in Saudi Arabia and a Qadaffi takes over or if you break Iran's image of being capable of resisting outside pressures, you're going to open up political trends which could defeat your economic objectives. Economic pressures or incentives, on the other hand, take time to organize and cannot be effective without consumer solidarity. Moreover, if we had created the political crisis that I described, we would almost certainly have had to do it against the opposition of Europe, Japan and the Soviet Union.

His interrogators persisted:

BUSINESS WEEK: Are there any political pressures the United States can bring to bear on the oil cartel?

KISSINGER: A country of the magnitude of the United States is never without political recourse. Certainly countries will have to think twice about raising their prices because it would certainly involve some political cost. But I don't want to go into this very deeply. . . .

BUSINESS WEEK: One of the things we . . . hear from businessmen is that in the long run the only answer to the oil cartel is some sort of military action. Have you considered military action on oil?

KISSINGER: Military action on oil prices?

BUSINESS WEEK: Yes.

KISSINGER: A very dangerous course. We should have learned from Vietnam that it is easier to get into a war than to get out of it. I am not saying that there's no circumstance where we would not use force. But it is one thing to use it in the case of a dispute over price, but it's another where there is some actual strangulation of the industrialized world.

BUSINESS WEEK: Do you worry about what the Soviets would do in the Middle East if there were any military action against the cartel?

KISSINGER: I don't think this is a good thing to speculate about. Any President who would resort to military action in the Middle East without worrying what the Soviets would do would have to be reckless. The question is to what extent he would let himself be deterred by it. But you cannot say you would not consider what the Soviets would do. I want to make clear, however, that the use of force would be considered only in the gravest emergency.[8]

Although he was prodded into this verbal exchange by his interviewers, there is no doubt that the Secretary of State said exactly what he intended to say. *Business Week* conducted the interview on December 23, and Kissinger reviewed the transcript on December 25, before it was published in the January 13, 1975, issue. When his carefully phrased references to remote possibilities when force might be considered caused a stir in Arab and European capitals, Kissinger claimed to be "astonished." He insisted on public television that "no nation can announce that it will let itself be strangled without reacting . . . I find it very difficult to see what it is that people are objecting to." He was simply saying that the United States would not permit itself or its allies to be strangled. "Somebody else would have to make the first move to attempt the strangulation. . . . There would have to be an overt move of an extremely drastic, dramatic and aggressive nature" before the United States would seriously consider using military forces against the oil producers.[9]

Only against economic actions that in their effects and intent would be akin to the use of force would the United States respond militarily; but in not totally ruling out such contingencies Kissinger obviously was attempting to warn the Arabs that at some point even their oil pricing policies, let alone another embargo, could seriously provoke the United States.

Kissinger was shown to be correct in characterizing these extreme possibilities as remote, for by 1975 the OPEC countries had begun to reconsider the consequences to themselves of price rises that would stimulate consumers to make substantial investments in alternate energy sources. But even discounting reckless economic or political power plays, it was evident to Kissinger and other Western statesmen that an important shift in the global balance of power was taking place, in that key nations in the Third World were able to crucially affect the security and well-being of most of the countries in the noncommunist industrialized world. Nor was the multiplier effect of the changed power equation lost on the majority of Third World leaders, who now saw a chance—as long as they acted as a bloc with the

OPEC countries—to make the West respond seriously to their longstanding demands for a better break in the world economy.

Kissinger was not at all pleased with the tacit bargain between the OPEC countries and other Third World countries to support one another's demands in international forums to maximize their bargaining leverage. Professedly nonaligned African, Latin American, and Asian nations now ganged up in the United Nations and its subsidiary organs to help the Arab countries pass anti-Israel resolutions. In return, the Middle Eastern Arab countries and Iran lent their support to some of the most radical demands emanating from the Third World for a restructuring of the international economic order and a global redistribution of income to the economically disadvantaged nations. "It is an irony," said Kissinger in an angry speech in July 1975,

> that at the moment the United States has accepted nonalignment and the value of diversity, those nations which originally chose this stance to preserve their sovereign independence from powerful military alliances are forming a rigid grouping of their own. The most solid bloc in the world today is, paradoxically, the alignment of the nonaligned. This divides the world into categories of North and South, developing and developed, imperial and colonial, at the very moment in history when such categories have become irrelevant and misleading.

He warned those now in the majority in the UN General Assembly and its specialized bodies not to operate under the illusion that they could use their voting power coercively without paying a large price, "for the coerced are under no obligation to submit. To the contrary, they are given all too many incentives simply to depart the scene, to have done with the pretense." Those who abuse the procedures of the organization to isolate or deny the full privileges of the United Nations to members they dislike, as the majority, prodded by the Arabs, was now doing to Israel, "may well inherit an empty shell."

The United States has been by far the largest supporter of the United Nations, Kissinger reminded the Third World voting bloc; but the support of the American people, which has been the lifeblood of the organization, will be profoundly alienated unless fair play predominates and the numerical majority respects the views of the minority. The American people are understandably tired of the inflammatory rhetoric against us, the all-or-nothing stance accompanied by demands for *our* sacrifice which too frequently dominate the meeting halls of the United Nations.[10]

As if to drive home his growing anger, Kissinger had President Ford appoint Daniel Patrick Moynihan as the new U.S. Ambassador to the United Nations. Moynihan had recently published in *Commentary* a scathing attack on the Third World advocates of a new international economic order, whom he lumped together as the "Fabian socialist" international party of "equality," and their apologists in the United States. The United States should take the offensive, argued Moynihan, as the leader of the "liberty party" and speak out loudly against those who would sacrifice freedom and condone tyranny in the pursuit of professedly egalitarian ends.[11]

Kissinger's hardening rhetoric and the appointment of Moynihan raised apprehension in UN circles about the Seventh Special Session of the General Assembly, scheduled for the fall of 1975. The Special Session was to consider means of implementing the principles of the "new international economic order" formulated by the General Assembly majority in the Charter of Economic Rights and Duties of States voted the previous December. The Third World coalition was demanding

—international commodity agreements to assure the producers of the Third World of remunerative and "equitable" prices, perhaps by indexing commodity prices to prices of manufactured goods.
—debt relief in the form of cancelation or postponement of the repayment obligations of the poor countries to their international creditors.
—preferential treatment for developing-country exports in the markets of the industrialized world.
—increased official development assistance from the rich

countries amounting to at least 0.7 percent of the gross national product of each rich country.

—increased allocations of special drawing rights (SDRs), the
International Monetary Fund's reserve assets created to al-
leviate the balance-of-payments deficits of member countries.

—technology transfers from the technologically advanced
countries to developing countries at concessionary prices.

—the right to nationalize and expropriate any foreign hold-
ings within their territories without compensation (a demand directed at the current *bête noire* of the Third World
militants, the multinational corporation).

—greater representation and voting rights for developing
countries in international funding and lending institutions.

To the relief of all countries, save perhaps the Soviet Union,
China, and some of the more intransigent Third World militants
such as Algeria and Libya, the feared North–South confrontation
failed to materialize. The big struggle took place before the convening of the Seventh Special Session, not between the diplomats of the industrial and developing nations but within the U.S.
government, between State Department officials sympathetic to
the demands of the Third World and Treasury officials anxious to
protect the international economic status quo. Kissinger was
converted to the reformist position sometime during the summer of 1975; and in the weeks immediately preceding the UN
meeting he reportedly was engaged in a major dispute with Secretary of the Treasury Simon over the official U.S. posture toward the Third World's demands for a new international economic order. Kissinger won out and, with the blessing of
President Ford, presented the new American policy to the
United Nations in his historic address of September 1, 1975. It
fell to Ambassador Moynihan, of all people, to deliver the Secretary of State's address to the General Assembly. (Moynihan, it
became clear in subsequent months, never bought the philosophy he was now instructed to expound.)

The specific proposals put forward in Kissinger's address to the Seventh Special Session went only part way toward meeting the grievances of the developing-country coalition; but they did imply substantial acceptance of the legitimacy of international compensations to the poorer countries for their comparative disadvantages in the international market.[12]

Granting the obligation of the international community to protect vulnerable economies against dramatic drops in their export earnings, Kissinger proposed the creation of a new "development security facility" within the IMF with the mandate and financial resources to give concessionary loans and grants to developing countries to make up for their export shortfalls. (However, the United States rejected the standing demand of the Third World militants for an indexing system to peg the price of basic commodities to price changes in industrial goods.)

Conceding that many of the poor countries, in all fairness, did deserve special help in raising development capital, Kissinger urged expansion of the lending programs of the World Bank and the regional development banks as well as the creation of an international investment trust to mobilize portfolio investment capital for local enterprises. In addition, the United States would be willing to provide technical assistance and expertise to developing countries ready to enter long-term capital markets, and asked other developed countries to provide similar assistance.

On the touchy issue of the role of multinational corporations, Kissinger recognized the concerns of many host countries regarding the ability of foreign-controlled firms to dominate their economies, evade local laws, and intervene in their politics. He affirmed that "countries are entitled to regulate the operations of transnational enterprises within their borders." But, contended Kissinger, host governments had an obligation to treat transnational enterprises equitably and responsibly: "Governments and enterprises must both respect the contractual obligations that they freely undertake. Contracts should be negotiated openly, fairly, and with full knowledge of their implications. . . . Factfinding and arbitral procedures must be promoted as means for settling international disputes."

Finally, with respect to developing-country demands for a greater role in international institutions and negotiations, Dr.

Kissinger agreed that "participation in international decisions should be widely shared, in the name of both justice and effectiveness . . . No country or group of countries should have exclusive power in areas basic to the welfare of others. This principle is valid for oil. It also applies to trade and finance."[13]

Kissinger was to experience frustration in his attempts to implement these proposals in the form of specific agreements between the developed and developing countries. In part, this was because of the lack of enthusiasm in the departments of Treasury and Commerce for the whole approach of responsiveness to Third World demands. In part, it was because of the lingering suspicion among Third World leaders of Kissinger's motives, their fear being that he wanted to split the developing-country coalition from the OPEC countries and was attempting to co-opt the poor militants with cosmetic generosity. But as Kissinger's policies toward Africa in 1976 were to show, there was a shift taking place in his grand strategy that was both fundamental and genuine.

Africa and the Realpoltik of Change

Departing from Andrews Air Force Base on April 23, 1976, the Secretary of State made a brief statement to the small group of ambassadors from the African countries he would visit on his trip. "The President has asked me to visit Africa to express the commitment of the United States to the interest in majority rule of the black African countries. . . . There are millions of Americans who have close cultural ties to Africa, and all Americans have ties of values and aspirations. I expect to express this when I visit Africa." There was only one exchange with a reporter before he boarded his plane:

> Q. *Mr. Secretary, in your meetings with African leaders, are you prepared to spell out point by point how the United States will match Soviet efforts in the African continent?*
> **SECRETARY KISSINGER:** We are not in Africa to match Soviet efforts. We are in Africa for our own purposes. I will indicate what our purposes are and what specific steps we are prepared to take.[14]

The media, not expecting the Kissinger trip to be anything more than a salvage operation after the humiliation of backing the losing side in the Angolan civil war, failed to catch the shift in U.S. policy telegraphed by his cryptic remarks on the runway. Four days later, at a luncheon hosted by President Kenneth Kaunda of Zambia, Kissinger, once again surprised the world with a bold recasting of U.S. policy on southern Africa, identifying the United States for the first time as unequivocally on the side of black majority rule.

The new U.S. policy that Kissinger outlined comprehensively in Lusaka on April 27, 1976, was clearly a dramatic turnabout from the assumptions of the so-called tar baby policy the Nixon administration had decided on during its first year in office. "Tar baby" was the second of five basic African policy options considered by the National Security Council between August 1969 and January 1970, when Kissinger made known his recommendations to the President. It was nicknamed "tar baby" by its State Department opponents to express their judgment that it was a sticky policy that the United States would be unable to abandon if it did not work. (In the famous Uncle Remus story by Joel Chandler Harris, Brer Fox makes a tar baby and sets it by the side of the road to trick Brer Rabbit. Brer Rabbit falls into the trap and gets completely stuck.)[15]

The first option considered by the NSC in 1969 (reflecting the views of former Secretary of State Dean Acheson, who had been urging such a policy on the President) called for "closer association with the white regimes to protect and enhance our economic, strategic, and scientific interests." It contemplated relaxation of the arms embargo against South Africa imposed during the Kennedy and Johnson administrations; resumption of routine U.S. naval visits and use of South Africa's military airfields; active promotion of U.S. exports to and direct investments in South Africa, South West Africa, and the Portuguese territories; relaxation of economic sanctions against Rhodesia; relaxation of the U.S. embargo on arms shipments to the Portuguese territories; and phasing out direct U.S. economic assistance to the black African states, relying instead on multilateral programs.[16]

Option two ("tar baby") called for "selective relaxation of our stance toward the white regimes" while maintaining a public posture of "opposition to racial repression." The policy was based explicitly on the premise that "the whites are here to stay and the only way that constructive change can come about is through them. There is no hope for the blacks to gain the political rights they seek through violence, which will only lead to chaos and increased opportunities for the communists." Increased U.S. economic aid would be provided to the black states "to focus their attention on their internal development and to give them a motive to cooperate in reducing tensions." The Republic of South Africa would also be encouraged to provide economic assistance to the black states of Africa. The NSC proponents of the policy pointed out its central implications:

> This option accepts, at least over a 3 to 5 year period, the prospect of unrequited U.S. initiatives toward the whites and some opposition from the blacks in order to develop an atmosphere conducive to change in white attitudes through persuasion and erosion. To encourage this change in white attitudes, we would indicate our willingness to accept political arrangements short of guaranteed progress toward majority rule, provided that they assure broadened political participation in some form by the whole population.

Concrete measures to implement the policy might include a selective liberalization of the arms embargo against South Africa and the Portuguese territories, plus other relaxations of sanctions against the white regimes similar to those recommended in connection with option one; and flexible aid programs for the black states, including "nonsophisticated arms" in response to "reasonable requests" but opposition to the use of force by insurgent movements.[17]

The third option was supposed to represent the policy inherited from the previous administration. This would involve continuing in the UN and in American bilateral relations to express basic opposition to the racial and colonial policies of the white states while retaining diplomatic, military, economic, and scientific relations with the white governments in ways "which do not imply our condoning of racial repression." However, the arms embargo against South Africa and the Portuguese territories would be strictly enforced, as would the economic sanctions against the Ian Smith regime in Rhodesia. The basic advantage of the inherited policy as seen by its supporters in the State Department was that, more than the other options, it preserved some flexibility for movement closer to either white or black states, depending on future developments.[18]

Options four and five were thrown in for consideration to round out the array of logical alternatives, not because there was any substantial advocacy for these positions within the administration. Four was a suggestion for the United States to simply cut its ties with the white regimes under the assumption that they would continue to resist constructive change no matter what the United States tried and that therefore increasing violence was unavoidable and the outcome would be—inevitably—black victory. Programs of assistance to the black governments would be continued and expanded, and the United States would open contact with African insurgent groups in the white-dominated states and express sympathy for their objectives. Option five was a complete hands-off policy toward the inevitably intensifying racial confrontation, under the assumption that its outcomes were unpredictable and that the United States was, in any case, incapable of affecting the course of events in southern Africa. It would be best, therefore, to maintain clean hands through a posture of scrupulous noninvolvement.[19]

In approving option two, the President set the direction for a U.S. course in southern Africa over the next five years that was to end ingloriously with the Angola crisis of 1975–1976. The United States got stuck on the tar of its policy of improving relations with the white regimes while the Soviets were left to pick and choose among black clients. Kissinger's first reponse to this larger geopolitical consequence of "tar baby" was to counterintervene "covertly" against the Soviets and the Cubans in Africa; but in Angola this only produced the further embarrassment of associating the United States with the losing blacks.

Angola provided the shock of recognition for Kissinger that

conservative realpolitik would no longer work in Africa. He resisted learning this lesson, however, until U.S. incompetence in Angola was exposed before the entire world.

Not that he wasn't warned. The Assistant Secretary of State for African Affairs, Nathaniel Davis, saw the handwriting on the wall and shared his judgement with the Secretary in no uncertain terms. Davis had been asked by Kissinger to chair an interagency NSC task force on Angola in the spring of 1975. The first job of the Task Force was to evaluate the latest request from the Central Intelligence Agency for a substantial increase in the covert support the agency was already providing to the opponents of Agostinho Neto and his Popular Movement for the Liberation of Angola (MPLA).

In January 1975 the CIA had been authorized by the Forty Committee (the top-level review board that controlled covert operations abroad during the Nixon and Ford administrations) to funnel $300,000 worth of assistance secretly to Neto's principal opponent, Holden Roberto, the leader of the National Front for the Liberation of Angola. The CIA was now back for more funds and for authorization to expand its political and economic assistance into covert military aid to counter the growing Soviet shipments of military equipment to Neto and his increasing reliance on Cuban military advisers in the escalating civil war. It was also asking for authorization to initiate a new program of support for another of Neto's opponents, Jonas Savimbi.

The CIA plan was strongly opposed by the NSC Task Force and by Assistant Secretary Davis. The Task Force's report, submitted to Kissinger in June 1975, pointed out that the covert military actions the CIA was recommending might lead to increased intervention by the Soviet Union and other foreign powers. The level of violence in Angola would probably increase and, especially if there were widespread tribal or racial massacres, U.S. support for one or more of the indigenous rivals would become a major political issue in the United States and an embarrassment internationally. It would be impossible to ensure that the CIA operations could be kept secret, concluded the Task Force, and their exposure would have a negative impact on US relations with many countries as well as with large segments of the U.S. public and Congress. Moreover, the United States would be committing its prestige in a situation over which it had limited influence and one whose outcome was highly uncertain. If the MPLA did come to power, the chances for the United States to establish workable relations with it would have been greatly damaged.[20]

Assistant Secretary Davis weighed in with his own memorandum against the CIA plan. To have even a slight chance of success, he argued, the United States would have to intervene in Angola with a much higher level of visibility and resources than that envisioned in the proposals for covert military operations. The CIA paper itself admitted that the Soviets enjoyed greater freedom of action in the covert supply of military equipment and could escalate the level of aid more readily than the United States. Davis implored the Forty Committee to face the implications:

> If we go in, we must go in quickly, massively and decisively enough to avoid the tempting, gradual, mutual escalation that characterized Vietnam during the 1965–67 period. . . . Unless we are prepared to go as far as necessary, in world balance of power terms the worst possible outcome would be a test of will and strength which we lose. The CIA paper makes clear that in the best of circumstances we won't be able to win. If we are to have a test of strength with the Soviets, we should find a more advantageous place.[21]

Davis' protestations were to no avail. The Forty Committee, with Kissinger's concurrence, endorsed the CIA Action Plan, and President Ford gave Kissinger and the CIA the go-ahead to implement it. Davis asked to be relieved of his position as Assistant Secretary of State for African affairs. This was in July 1975. Over the next six months, virtually all of Davis' predictions came true. The Soviets transported over 10,000 Cuban troops into Angola by air and sea and flew in massive amounts of combat equipment for use by the Cubans and the MPLA, while South Africa and Zaïre intervened against Neto's forces. In December the Senate voted to prohibit all further covert aid to Angola. The Soviets and the Cubans pressed their advantage. Neto trounced his opponents in the northern regions of Angola, who had been aided by forces from Zaïre. The South Africans withdrew their forces from the southern regions of Angola. By the end of January 1976, it was all over except the recriminations.

On January 29, 1976, Kissinger appeared before the Subcommittee on African Affairs of the Senate Committee on Foreign Relations in one last defense of his Angola policies. The blame for their failure, he insisted, lay not with the Ford administration but with Congress for failing to provide the wherewithal for standing up to the Russians in the crunch. His testimony was a string of castigations of the congressional majority for their naiveté and lack of spine:

> Military aggression, direct or indirect, has frequently been successfully dealt with, but never in the absence of a local balance of forces. U.S. policy in Angola has sought to help friends achieve this balance. Angola represents the first time since the aftermath of World War II that the Soviets have moved militarily at long distances to impose a regime of their choice. It is the first time that the U.S. has failed to respond to Soviet military moves outside their immediate orbit. And it is the first time that Congress has halted the Executive's action when it was in the process of meeting this kind of threat. . . .
>
> If the United States is seen to emasculate itself in the face of massive, unprecedented Soviet and Cuban intervention, what will be the perception of leaders around the world as they make decisions concerning their future security? . . .
>
> I must note with some sadness that by its actions the Congress has deprived the President of indispensable flexibility in formulating a foreign policy which we believe to be in our national interest. And Congress has ignored the crucial truth that a stable relationship with the Soviet Union based on mutual restraint will be achieved only if Soviet lack of restraint carries the risk of counteraction. . . .
>
> Our diplomacy was effective so long as we maintained the leverage of a possible military balance. African determination to oppose Soviet and Cuban intervention was becoming more and more evident. . . .
>
> By mid-December we were hopeful that the [Organization of African Unity] would provide a framework for eliminating the interference of outside powers by calling for an end to their intervention.

At that point, the impact of our domestic debate overwhelmed the possibilities of diplomacy. After the Senate vote to block any further aid to Angola, the Cubans more than doubled their forces and Soviet military aid was resumed on an even larger scale. The scope of Soviet–Cuban intervention increased drastically; the cooperation of Soviet diplomacy declined.[22]

Senator Dick Clark, chairman of the subcommittee on African Affairs, disagreed profoundly. The important lesson of Angola, he maintained, is that we should not ignore the African black liberation movements until their victories against the minority regimes are imminent and then back particular factions simply because their opponents are backed by the Soviet Union. The United States, urged Senator Clark, should make a new beginning in its African policy. It should be directed toward establishing connections between U.S. and African commitments to human rights and racial equality and between the U.S. commitment to international pluralism and African concepts of nonalignment. If the United States pursues such a new African policy, contended Clark, "our cold war interests in Africa may very well take care of themselves."[23]

In February the Organization of African Unity—the all-African regional association of black states—officially recognized the Neto regime as the legitimate government of Angola. Kissinger said little about Africa in public during the next two months. Only when he unveiled his new African policy in Lusaka at the end of April was it evident that he had taken to heart some of the criticisms leveled at him by Senator Clark and others.

He had come to Africa, he said, "to usher in a new era in American policy." This new American policy endorsed the black African premise that racial justice and majority rule were the prerequisites for peace in Africa. This endorsement, however, was "not simply a matter of foreign policy but an imperative of our own moral heritage."

Specifically, with respect to Rhodesia, the United States unequivocally supported the British insistence that independence was illegal unless it was based on majority rule. "The Salisbury regime must understand," Kissinger warned, "that it cannot expect U.S. support either diplomatically or in material help at any stage in its conflict with African states or African liberation movements. On the contrary, it will face our unrelenting opposition until a negotiated settlement [to institute majority rule] is achieved." Accordingly, the United States was taking steps to insure its own and other nations' strictest compliance with UN resolutions on economic sanctions against Rhodesia. Consistent with U.S. nonrecognition of the Ian Smith regime in Salisbury, "American travelers will be advised against entering Rhodesia. American residents there will be asked to leave." In addition, the United States was ready to provide special economic assistance to countries bordering on Rhodesia that might themselves suffer economic hardship as a result of closing their borders to normal trade with Rhodesia. The Ford administration was prepared to immediately provide $12.5 million to Mozambique under this policy. Looking toward a successful transition to majority rule in Rhodesia and then full independence, Kissinger promised that the United States would join other nations in a program of economic and technical assistance to the "newly independent Zimbabwe." (Kissinger's use of the black African name for the country was symbolic of the basic shift in policy he was attempting to convey.) While essentially deferring to the blacks to establish their own regime in their own way, Kissinger nevertheless found it necessary to state "our conviction that whites as well as blacks should have a secure future and civil rights in a Zimbabwe that has achieved racial justice. A constitutional structure should protect minority rights together with establishing majority rule."

On the Namibia question, Kissinger strongly reiterated the standing U.S. position that the Republic of South Africa's continued occupation of its former mandate territory was illegal and that the South African government should withdraw and allow the United Nations to supervise the Namibian people's attainment of full self-determination and independent statehood.

On the matter of South Africa's internal racial policies, Kissinger associated the United States with the position of the black African states more clearly than any previous top U.S. official had. "The world community's concern with South Africa is not merely that racial discrimination exists there," said Kissinger. "What is unique is the extent to which racial discrimination has been institutionalized, enshrined in law, and made all-pervasive." The right of the white South Africans to live in their country was not being challenged by the world community, observed Kissinger. But the white South Africans must realize that the world will not tolerate the continued institutionalized separation of the races being enforced under the "apartheid" policy. Pretoria must heed the warning signals of recent years. "There is still time to bring about a reconciliation of South Africa's peoples for the benefit of all. But there is a limit to that time—a limit of far shorter duration than was generally perceived even a few years ago." In the immediate future the black African nations and the world community would be judging Pretoria's legitimacy as an African nation not only from its efforts to make constructive progress toward the elimination of apartheid but also from its behavior on the Namibian and Rhodesian issues. "The Republic of South Africa can show its dedication to Africa," advised Kissinger, "by using its influence in Salisbury to promote a rapid negotiated settlement for majority rule in Rhodesia."[24]

The Secretary of State backed up his new political orientation toward African issues by pledging to triple U.S. economic support for development programs in southern and central Africa over the next three years. And he gave this new stance additional credibility by stopping in Nairobi, Kenya, on the way back from his southern African tour to address the United Nations Conference on Trade and Development—the main UN forum through which the Third World countries had been pressing their demands—on how the United States was prepared to implement in detail the new approach to North–South economic issues that he had outlined the previous fall at the Seventh Special Session of the United Nations.

The evolution of Kissinger's North–South policy—now focused primarily on Africa—was remarkably analogous to the evolution in U.S. Latin American policy associated with the Kennedy administration's Alliance for Progress. It took the failure of a too little, too late intervention against the "communist threat" in Cuba (climaxed by the ill-fated Bay of Pigs invasion by Cuban exiles organized by the CIA) to convince the Kennedy administration that an entirely new approach that would put the United States on the side of progressive social change in Latin America was the only hope for arresting the growth of Soviet influence in the western hemisphere. Similarly, Kissinger's futile and tardy effort to salvage the Angola situation turned him in the direction of a type of alliance for progress in Africa as the best means of containing the expanding Soviet presence. In both cases a cold war motive lay in back of the programs, but the public definition of the program and its principal instrumentalities were cast in terms of economic and political development objectives. Kissinger would not like this analogy. He had vituperatively criticized Kennedy's Alliance for Progress as naive in its premise that democratic socialists rather than the conservative military elite of the Third World would provide the best bulwark against instability and Soviet attempts to capture leftist movements. Now he was embracing movements and concepts that he had previously branded as romantic and soft, as insufficiently based on hard balance-of-power realities to be able to effectively counter the unsentimental and often brutal Marxist–Leninists.

"Has Henry lost his nerve?" asked critics on the right. "Is he merely up to his old deceptive tricks?" asked critics on the left. Perhaps both suppositions were wrong. Perhaps he believed it was time for a higher realpolitik: to advance, as he told the UN General Assembly, "from the management of crises to the building of a more stable and just international order—an order resting not on power but on restraint of power, not on the strength of arms but on the strength of the human spirit."[25]